Stage Combat

Stage

Fisticuffs, Stunts,
Combat
and Swordplay

Jenn Zuko Boughn

for Theater and Film

ALLWORTH PRESS
NEW YORK

10   09   08   07   06   5   4   3   2   1

Published by Allworth Press
An imprint of Allworth Communications, Inc.
10 East 23rd Street, New York, NY 10010

Cover design by Derek Bacchus
Interior design by Dianna Little
Page composition/typography by Susan Ramundo
Cover photo by Ginger Zukowski

ISBN-13: 978-1-58115-461-0
ISBN-10: 1-58115-461-5

Library of Congress Cataloging-in-Publication Data
Boughn, Jenn Zuko.
    Stage combat: fisticuffs, stunts, and swordplay for theater and film/Jenn Zuko Boughn.
        p.   cm.
    Includes bibliographical references and index.
    1. Stage fighting.   I. Title.

PN2071.F5B68   2006
792.02'8—dc22
                                    2006026840

Printed in Canada

Dedication

For Mom, my first movement instructor, and Jason,
my current movement instructor, with love

Contents

Acknowledgments

I'm honored and proud to have been involved with so many extraordinary, talented people, who all added to making this project fun and successful.

Thanks to Timothy Tait, Dale Girard, and Geoff Kent for introducing me to, training me for, and continuing to play with me in the SAFD stage combat world. Also to the theatre companies of the University of Colorado, Boulder; Frequent Flyers Productions; and Five Funny Faces for support, training, and theatrical brilliance over the years.

To the Genki Kai and the Boulder Quest Center, two dynamite martial arts groups. Your high quality training is appreciated. To Jason Boughn, for throwing a dagger into my throat and then my heart. I'm proud to be his wife and *uchi-deshi*.

To Ginger and Jesse Zukowski for being superhuman amateur photographers, and thanks also to Cynthia Berry for her aerial dance pictures from back in the day! Huge thanks to Jesse and Jason for being enthusiastic, hardworking models. And thanks to Nicole, Derek, and everyone at Allworth Press for putting it all together and making it pretty!

Finally, I'd like to thank the Metropolitan State College of Denver's theatre program for putting up the class every year, and especially the inaugural fall 2005 semester Fundamentals of Stage Combat class. You guys were fabulous students and models as well. I look forward to Metro's stage combat class every year—thanks for making it such a pleasure the first time around.

Caution!

Do not mess about or play carelessly with any of the techniques, drills, or exercises you see in this book.

Though the manual is set up for easy reference and explanation for the beginner, you should never undertake any physical activity (particularly illusions of violence) without prior consultation of a doctor. This manual is meant as a guide and an addition to, not a substitute for, professional instruction. Use the techniques, drills, and exercises with caution, care, and professional guidance or supervision. Those involved with the writing, research, and production of this book are not responsible for any injury while practicing anything found within.

The photographs herein represent both experts and beginners in the field of stage combat: the mix of depicted skill levels is meant for inspiration both to the experienced practitioner and to the beginning student who may think she's too klutzy for stage combat.

Chapter One

Violence and Actor Safety

We've all no doubt heard it said that artists "suffer for their art." Artists in general have a certain masochistic reputation among layfolk: How many times have we researched a poet's or an actor's biography, only to discover years of substance abuse and emotional problems? And there are countless stories of actors involved in messy divorces or doing a rehab stint. So actors themselves have this idea that they are giant puppets made to show suffering onstage for entertainment—if they themselves suffer for the performance, so much the better for authenticity.

The Show Doesn't Have to Go On

There was a memorable story posted on the bulletin board in the University of Denver theatre department that ran approximately like this:[1] At a college in Texas, a production of *Dracula* called for a scene in which Dracula was to be killed by driving a knife through his heart. The director came up with this brilliant solution: A stiff panel was rigged underneath the vampire's shirt. The actor stabbing him then used a real bowie knife, stabbing the

sharp, unretractable blade into the guard panel, thereby allowing for a realistic stabbing without hurting the actor being stabbed. Of course, theatre being the unpredictable art that it is, one night the panel had shifted, and the actor playing Dracula was stabbed in the chest. He recovered in the hospital from a punctured lung, and proceeded to sue the university soon thereafter.

What's the point of bringing up this anecdote? Simple: There is *no reason* for an actor to be in that kind of danger onstage. There is *no justification* for real violence onstage. Hiring a trained fight coordinator may seem like an unnecessary expense, especially in a small theatre with a minuscule budget, but without stage combat choreography, serious problems can occur. Even a simple pratfall or slap in the face can cause real damage to an actor if not done properly. And if done properly, it loses none of its realism for an audience. Any actor who tells you he'd rather actually be slapped in a scene instead of learn a stage slap because of authenticity[2] should learn the following unlucky thirteen:

1. Catching the eyeball with a fingernail can cause permanent blindness or a dislocated lens, not to mention serious pain in the moment.

2. A stray fingernail can rip the eyelid, lip, or other tender parts on the face.

3. Covering the ear with a slapping hand can cause a miniature vacuum in the ear canal, which can rupture the eardrum, causing permanent deafness.

4. Slapping the ear with an open hand can cause "cauliflower ear," a common disfigurement seen in boxers.

5. It takes a modest clap to dislocate the jaw.

6. It takes a strong clap to break the collarbone.

7. If earrings are worn, there are potential rip or puncture hazards. If rings are worn, the face or anything on it can be torn.

8. Not to mention a basic lost contact lens or glasses gone to the floor or askew, which is disconcerting in the middle of a scene.

9. Or a bloody nose, which stops the action, scares an audience, and ruins costumes.

10. Just a little adrenaline (which we all have when onstage) can cause the "victim" to bite her tongue or lip.

11. Just a little more adrenaline than the above example can knock out a tooth.

12. Ever have a broken nose? The pain and shiners will put you out of work for a while. If part of your nose's bone is driven into the brain, you could suffer internal facial bleeding (yuck), or even, in extreme cases, brain damage or death.

13. The temple is a tender spot, and you can suffer brain damage or death if it is struck with force.[3]

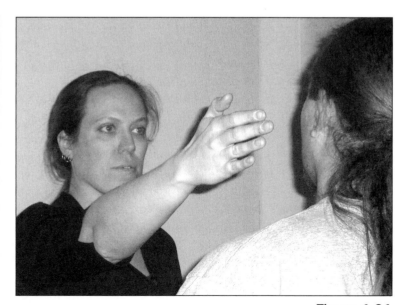

Figure 1.01

Obviously, this list of serious slap-related injuries doesn't even include the simple bruising or scratching that can occur when one has to do a slap every night of every weekend for several weeks.

An actor's face is his résumé—he can't afford to look wounded, let alone be wounded, when at work. A basic stage slap uses no contact to the face at all, and in fact looks incredibly real to an audience when done correctly. (See figure 1.01.) An actor who can't "act" a fake slap (if taught proper technique) should perhaps reconsider his commitment to the scene.

It's Not as Easy as Falling off a Log

These days, a naturalistic, or method, style of acting is considered the best—the more realistic, the better. In fact, reality TV pushes the boundaries between entertainment and day-to-day life even further by using nonactors and actual contests instead of fictional drama (or at least, that's the premise—really the characters on reality TV are auditioned, cast, and directed as much as those in a sitcom). Therefore, the in-depth training and craft required for an actor to produce a quality performance is little known, if not disbelieved, by viewers of theatre. If it seems real, it is real. If the actors act naturally, well, who can't do that? They're just "being natural"; who needs a class or a degree or a mastery of an art just to be natural?

In truth, to act naturally onstage in front of many people (or a film crew and camera) takes quite a bit of training, not the least of which is to start from scratch as far as discovering what rings true to an audience member. It is possible for an actor giving an authentic performance to run around the block three times in order to appear winded as she enters a scene, but why? Since theatre by definition is not real life, but an artifice put up on a stage for entertainment and educational purposes, isn't there a way an actor can "put on" the authentic windedness for her performance without being literal?

As stated in the previous section, there is no reason for an actor to be hurt onstage, not for authenticity's sake, not for any reason. There should also be no excuse for an actor to settle for a fake-looking bit of violence, which not only jars the *audience* out of the moment, but the *actor* as well. Quality stage combat provides the best of both worlds: The violence looks real to an audience, plays real for an actor's intentions, and keeps everyone onstage safe at all times.

The purpose of this manual is to provide the techniques and philosophy required for grasping the fundamentals of a growing theatrical art: stage combat. These techniques can be used by any theatre practitioner, but of course, hiring a stage combat professional is always the best way to go. Using this manual as a complement to instruction by a qualified professional will ensure better safety and detailed technique, especially for the beginner. Finally, as is true with any movement system, *be careful* and don't mess around with this stuff at home. Though "fake," stage combat is still dangerous and should be used professionally by professionals.

What You'll Need

The "practice journal" thing you'll read about through this chapter is my idea—mainly because theatre is such an ethereal

Note:

Yes, you are a stud muffin. You don't need to prove it. You may even know tons of historical information regarding weaponry and combat systems of bygone ages and be able to recite the exact combat maneuvers of the Battle of Agincourt. However, beating on yourself and your buddies with a sword (padded or no) isn't tough, it's stupid. Trust me, admirers appreciate skill and a whole skin, not dummies who prove their bad-assness through self-mutilation. Besides, unless you really know your market, most blades you buy are extraordinarily dangerous, not meant for anything but lovely wall decoration.[4] I'm talking to you, historical reenactors, convention-goers, live role-players, and Renaissance Faire patrons. Don't say I didn't warn you.

art, it is important to have some kind of reference point when researching a new skill, to keep details and personal experiences for later use. I recommend keeping a practice journal for all this stuff, including choreography and script notes later. Trust me, you'll want to reference them throughout your career. As a rule, having journal time at the end of each class/fight rehearsal is a good idea—that way, you can take time to write out what you've done, whether it's choreography or exercises for practice. Then take some time also to convene and discuss what you've done that day: how it feels, if there are any finesse questions, any final tips/pointers from the teacher or fight director.

Dress Code for Stage Combat Work: Obviously, when you are training for fight scenes and practicing by engaging in movement exercises, you should wear clothing that does not constrict you in any way and that allows for full body movement and won't fall off you if you go upside down. Some more specifics:

- No jeans!

- Either go barefoot (recommended) or wear proper studio shoes. No street shoes, no socks alone. This actually will depend on the floor being used. When on a dance floor, always go barefoot *except* when using weapons.

- Keep good hygiene; you will be working physically together constantly. Keep clean and good-smelling as a courtesy to those around you. Keep fingernails and toenails short for safety's sake.

- Keep long hair out of your eyes.

- No jewelry. This is a safety issue. Tiny earrings are okay, nothing else.

- Those with glasses: Either strap them onto your head or wear contacts.

---

[1] Brock Read, "Stage Combat in the News," *The Ring of Steel*, *www.deathstar.org/groups/ros/reference/news.html*.

[2] I actually heard this uttered by the star of a musical I was in, and the director opted not to use stage combat for the scene. One night, the actor did get clocked hard in the face, throwing his scene off for the night. Luckily, he suffered no permanent damage.

[3] Geoff Kent and Timothy Tait, personal communication through various, sundry lectures and demonstrations, 1996–1998.

[4] We'll go over safe stage sword requirements in chapter 6.

Chapter Two

Movement Awareness

The most important thing you can master regarding movement onstage is *awareness*. Simple? Not really—especially regarding combat and violence situations. Stage picture, appealing movement patterns, authentic action, actual combat skills, rhythm, etc., all add up to a seamless movement series onstage. You will make your director's job easier by having a basic movement awareness already there. Your impulses and natural ability to move with others will create organic stage pictures and movements, which will enhance any director's blocking or choreographer's designs.

Things to keep in mind, whether you are the actor who fights or a bystander: How comfortable is my character around the others, and how does this affect my body language around them? What is my character's relationship to weapons—am I a soldier, warrior, civilian? Do I regularly carry a weapon on my person? What and how large? What is my reaction when a weapon is drawn? Have I ever been in a physical confrontation? Am I a perpetrator? What is my character's *status* onstage?

The World Doesn't Actually Revolve around You

Picture this: an old miser and his crafty servant. A town mayor and his advisor. A battered wife and her abusive husband. A hillbilly and a proper Englishman. A queen gets knocked on her ass by a beggar. A king orders his brother beheaded. A young gang member pulls a gun on a child. A man challenges his best friend to a duel to the death. What does each of these phrases say about *status*?

What is status, anyway? Well, think about this: You are walking down a somewhat crowded, though safe, city street. Do you stare directly into the eyes of everyone you pass? Do you glance at a passerby, then lower your gaze? How many times do you make way for a person passing? Do you ever shoulder anyone out of the way? Every day, every moment, humans engage in status-play (unconsciously) in order to establish a basic functional pecking order. Humans are social animals, and status is as essential to us as it is to wolves in a pack. As rational beings, it just takes a bit more effort for us to be aware of what we're doing. Every smile, every crossing of the arms, every moment of eye contact or lack thereof, serves to establish a clear social order, without which society does not function.[1]

The effectiveness of a scene depends on the manipulation of the characters' status. Comedy ensues when there are large status gaps (the queen getting bowled over by the beggar), or when the audience does not feel sympathy for He Who Gets Slapped. If you are producing a comedy, you can have a king smack his valet, but only if the valet indicates to the audience that he's not in actuality the lower rank in *status*. The valet may get slapped, but then perhaps makes a face at the king behind his back. The audience will laugh, because this insult shows that a) the valet is not in fact hurt, and b) the king must be either foolish or weak, which of course means his status is low, regardless of title, wealth, etc.

Cartoons and Charlie Chaplin are prime examples of this. If the valet shows real pain, the audience may feel sorry for his lowly status and then think the scene is sick, not funny at all. Make sure you know what you're doing when you choose blocking—pay attention to the status happening onstage. Otherwise, you'll get laughs in a poignant moment, or shocked silence when you want a laugh.[2]

Status Exercise #1: Status Walks

Walk around the space; experiment with different ways of walking: on tiptoes, crouching, limping, erect, shambling, fast, slow, lopsided . . . the possibilities are endless. Once you've tried a bunch of different walks, begin interacting with the others around you. This is a nonverbal exercise, so keep sound to a minimum, concentrating on just the physical interaction. Spend several seconds to a couple minutes with each "character" you find. Afterward, journal and discuss your findings. How did you react to each "character," and can you pinpoint the *status* within each interaction? What were the most interesting encounters? The most stagnant? Once you've taken time to notice and discuss status after these encounters, do the exercise again. This time,

Figure **2.01**

notice the status that happens and *change it*, again using a minimum of sound and no words. After doing this a bunch of times, convene again and discuss: What did you do to change the status of your encounters? What does it mean to a scene to raise or lower one's own status as opposed to another's?

Status Exercise #2: Scene Status Change

Think about plays you've worked on or know well—what do the characters within these plays do to each other's status? If you are working on scenes now, take a few and try playing with status within them: lowering your own status, convincing your partner to lower his, raising your partner's or your own status . . . you get the idea. How to do this? Some easy ways to change status are as follows: a) lower your gaze/look at the floor (low), b) do not touch your face or move your head (high), c) praise the features, feats, etc., of your partner (high), d) admit you are not learned, attractive, etc., (low), e) pepper your speech with many short "ums" (low) . . . the list goes on. Experiment with improvised scenes and have observers notice and share what the status exchange is like.

A scene can change completely depending on status. As you experiment, decode and decide—which status pairing works the best for your scene? How should the status of the characters change to ideally show the movement of the dramatic action?

How does the subtext of the lines change depending on status? Surprise yourself—a stereotypical status exchange may work, but unusual matchings can work even better.

Detective Columbo (the famous television character played by Peter Falk) is a good study for a character who uses self-lowering to much advantage. With affable manner, wrinkled raincoat, absentminded ways, and slow prattle, Columbo will bring a person (the murderer) into his confidence: He'll admire his money, fame, fancy learning, or car, or if the person is a celebrity, he'll declare his wife is a big fan and even ask for an autograph. The more Columbo lowers his own status and raises that of the murderer, the more lax, confident, and careless the murderer becomes, until finally, the fatal slipup occurs and we see how masterful Columbo's status-play has been to cause the high-status character to finally topple.[3]

A classic physical example of status illustration is at the end of the initial rapier fight between Inigo and Westley in the film *The Princess Bride*. Westley stands straight upright, moving only his wrist to circle just the tip of his blade. Inigo clutches his one-handed sword with both hands, knees bent and back slightly contracted, head and arms jerkily and frantically attempting to follow Westley's sword-circles. This simple difference in stature and movement shows a viewer exactly who is about to win the fight.[4]

Status Exercise #3: The Hats Game[5]

The Hats Game is a fun way to discover and experiment with status as it happens between natural characters onstage. The rules are as follows: Four actors go at a time. Arrange them in rank order—one being the top rank, four being the bottom. All four actors have soft hats on. The physical action is that you're allowed to take the hat of anyone of a lower rank than you. If you do, you must throw the hat at the owner's feet. That's it. Grab hat, toss at feet.

Now, Number One can obviously take anyone's hat but would rather take Number Two's. Number Two can take anyone's but Number One's, but prefers to take Number Three's, and so on. Number Four can take no one's hat. How does he deal with his frustration?

Give the Hats Game a simple improvised scene: an executive chef and three sous-chefs attempting to prepare a meal, four friends packing up for a road trip or screwing in a light bulb, etc. Just such a simple series of rules can lead to hilarious results! Make it a boss-and-three-toadies scene, and add the following restriction: Each actor can speak only to his immediate superior, and is too good to speak to anyone lower than his immediate inferior.

Ensemble

You are not the only one onstage, so being aware of the people around you is essential. You should be able to gauge how much of the audience's attention you should be commanding at any time, based on your character. Don't rely only on the director to do this for you—you should know whether you're inappropriately stealing a scene or fading too far into the background, and you should also know where you are in relation to your scene-mates, to your *ensemble*.

Ensemble Exercise #1: Machines

You can make a movement machine for anything: a friendship machine, a sports machine, a machine to illustrate systems like a circuit, or a heart machine, a digestive system machine . . . again, the options are endless. The making of a machine is simple: One person starts by making a repetitive movement and sound. Then, one at a time, other members of the ensemble add their repetitive movement/sound, making sure that each new "gear" connects somehow to the whole. The "one at a time" rule is important because each player should take the time to assess the whole picture before adding herself to the mix.

The results are fun as well as fodder for a stage picture. You can even make machines appropriate for themes within your scene: a dueling machine, a lust machine, a chasing machine. Experiment with the abstract motions, then discuss: How does this goofy game relate to actual movement between people? Does this teach us anything about physical harmony onstage? Try taking a scene that actors are working on and use machines to block or choreograph the movements needed for it.

Ensemble Exercise #2: Eight-Counts

Each actor finds a spot A and a spot B in the space. Make sure each actor's two spots are easily located. Then, on cue, each actor takes a slow eight-count to travel (however she wishes) from her point A to her point B. Then each takes seven counts to travel from her point B back to her point A, and hold the eighth count. In the next round, the actors travel from A to B once again, only this time they take six counts to move, and hold beats seven and eight. This goes on in this way until they have to travel in one count and hold counts two through eight. Especially with these last two turns, the actors will really get a sense of traveling their own path with acute awareness of the others in the space with them (or collide!).[6]

Ensemble Exercise #3: Mirrors

Start out with the classic partnered mirror exercise: each partner sitting or on knees, mirroring gestures. Then, move the mirror movements to the feet. Make sure to switch leaders. Then, add words or sound (this will be challenging). Remember, you are mirrors, not mimics; every action and sound must happen *simultaneously*, even though one is the leader. Mirrors done in a large ensemble can be a good challenge as well—put some partners across the room from each other, some close together. How does this positioning affect partner mirror dynamics, as well as the dynamics of the whole space? Try large-group mirrors, with one leader and several followers. (See figures 2.02 and 2.03.)

Figure **2.02**

Figure **2.03**

Distancing

Of course, any of the above awareness exercises will show an actor some fundamentals of *distancing*, but one cannot stress enough how important good awareness of distance is in stage combat, armed or unarmed. Proper distance can mean the difference between realism and absurd fakery, or between "hospital, no hospital"[7] for the actor.

Distancing Exercise #1: Awareness 1[8]

With a partner, determine who is the mover, who is the sensor. The sensor should stand comfortably with plenty of space around himself, eyes closed; the mover should stand a few feet in front of the sensor, also relaxed and breathing easily. The mover then lifts a hand and leans forward, advancing slowly to touch the sensor. When the sensor feels the mover's advancing contact, he should raise his hand. The mover then freezes, and the sensor can open his eyes to see the distance and positioning of his partner. Make sure you switch roles.

Remember, the idea of this exercise is not to try to sneak up on your partner, or surprise him. It is not a contest—it is an exercise meant to teach natural distancing between people, and how we sense space. Also, it should teach the actor something about the size of his own personal space. Keep your pace uneven and slow, and take notes in a practice journal when you are done to keep track of your findings.

Distancing Exercise #2: Awareness 2[9]

This exercise is similar to the first, and should be done with medium- to small-sized groups. The sensor stands in the middle of a room with closed eyes, and the rest of the group positions themselves around her in a circle, a few feet away and evenly spaced. Once the group sees that the sensor is relaxed and breathing deeply, they silently choose which actor will be the first mover. The mover then extends his arm and leans forward slowly (just as in the previous exercise), attempting to touch the sensor. Once the sensor senses the incoming contact, she should point in the direction from which she thinks it's coming. When she points, the mover should freeze, and the sensor can see how accurate she was, then close her eyes and resume the game. Again, move slowly and switch movers at an uneven pace, so that the sensor doesn't become accustomed to a certain rhythm or pattern of movement. Change sensors so all actors get a chance to be the sensor. Record your experience in your practice journal.

Distancing Exercise #3: Peripheral Vision

The sensor stands about halfway to three-quarters of the way down in the middle of a room. The two movers start at the back of the room, one on either side of the sensor. The sensor keeps her focus soft and forward, eyes still. The movers advance slowly and silently forward. When the sensor sees either mover, she should point at him. The idea is to see how far your peripheral vision actually extends. Again, movers are not to try to surprise or sneak up on the receiver: Just move slowly and steadily, and freeze when you get "the finger." You can extend this exercise by adapting the movers into "attackers": Each attacker slowly works her way forward, this time separately and with projected intention, maybe even an extended hand to touch the sensor. The moment the sensor feels or sees an attacker, she should move appropriately to avoid the contact sensed.

Distancing Exercise #4: Projectile Evasion

Using a Nerf crossbow and an assortment of light plastic lids,[10] arrange the group sporadically around the space, and let 'em rip! The actors should try to evade the projectiles using as little movement as possible—try to avoid wild spasms or huge dives. Those who are hit should do pushups, crunches, or other torture of a set amount before they are allowed back in the fray. If an actor is hit three times, he is out for the round! This exercise is fantastic for spatial awareness for any age, from five-year-old children to high schoolers to adult martial-arts students. Its distancing skill-building is essential, and above all, it's fun!

Here are some rule variations to try, for variety and more precision evasion training:

Hira No Kamae: Stand upright with arms outstretched at head level. To evade, pivot either foot forward or backward, so that you face the "archer" sideways. (See figure 2.04.)

I Am Bruce Lee: Instead of evading the projectiles, attempt to catch them. If one hits the hand and falls, you're hit. If you catch a projectile successfully, switch places with one of the "archers."

Figure **2.04**

One More Note about Distancing:

Finding your distance onstage before (or during) set stage combat is essential for both realism and safety. Proper distancing in any technique can make or break the effect of the move, and certainly is the difference between injury and safety. Be sure to review the proper combat distancing for each weapon and non-weapon technique in this manual—proper distancing will be covered at the beginning of each chapter, and sometimes before each specific technique. Don't ignore such distance standards and exercises as unimportant; they should be practiced as much as (if not more than) the choreography itself. Once an actor has an ability to move into and out of safe distance smoothly, fights will look great and be safe at all times.

---

[1]   For more on status, read *Impro* by Keith Johnstone.

[2]   Also, speaking during a fight is generally comedic; silence during a fight is usually dramatic.

[3]   William Link and Richard Levinson created the Columbo character in 1971.

[4]   Reiner, dir., *The Princess Bride*, 1987.

[5]   Johnstone, *Impro: Improvisation and the Theatre*, 68–70.

[6]   Joyce Morgenroth, *Dance Improvisations*, 80–81.

[7]   Timothy Tait, Personal communication, from SAFD certification classes, 1996–7. Dale Girard likes to say, "Air don't bleed," which I like as well.

[8]   Hayes, *Ninja, Spirit of the Shadow Warrior*, 116–119.

[9]   Hayes, *Ninja, Spirit of the Shadow Warrior*, 122–123.

[10]   Lids can be saved from anything from Pringles cans to yogurt containers to anything else you can think of that can be thrown like little Frisbees. If a Nerf crossbow is unavailable, merely throwing foam balls or Wiffle balls works. Keep in mind the dynamic difference between a foam arrow and a Wiffle ball, and use such rhythm variety to your advantage.

Chapter Three

Taihenjutsu

The **Japanese word *taihenjutsu* means**, roughly, "body-movement techniques." In the Japanese martial arts, taihenjutsu includes rolls, falls, jumps, walks, and runs, as well as basic acrobatics meant mainly for evasion purposes. The following series of techniques will cover the ways in which an actor can (without injury) fall, roll, and otherwise go *kersplat* onstage. All of these techniques, when learned properly, look real (or spectacularly unreal, if that's the choreography choice) and cause the actor no injury at all. However, a stage surface is rarely made of mats, so for an actor to successfully roll or fall on a hard surface, certain stretching and maintenance is essential. In fact, stretching and limbering exercises are important for any actor, even those not taking pratfalls and such: A prepared body means a prepared mover onstage, not to mention a centered vocal apparatus (but that's another manual).

When dealing with an unskilled body, be sure you go slowly and softly, even using mats for the initial learning process, if available. Then, when you are accustomed to the contact and care needed for falls and rolls on a hard surface, gradually increase the speed

until you are at "stage speed." When using a technique or choreography for a show, *be sure to rehearse* the physical business at half-speed before every performance. Failure to do so can result in fudging and approximation, which equal danger for the actors (no matter how much they think they know what they're doing).

Stretching and Warm-Ups

These are only a selection of a multitude of different ways to stretch and strengthen the body in preparation for intense physical activity. Any dance or movement training or any physical therapist's regimen will give you great stretching exercises as well. Keep in mind that any stretch should be sustained, not bouncy—to preserve the muscle structure and guard against pulls—and held for at least fifteen to thirty seconds straight, or the muscles will snap right back to where they were and the stretch won't do any good. Be sure to engage each movement in your abdomen, using core strength more than peripheral muscle effort. Oh, and don't forget to *breathe*![1]

Stretching Positions #1

Tuck: Tuck position (as in fig. 3.01), imagining a bowling ball held on the belly. Balance on the sit-bones, roll down the spine without letting go the bowling ball. Balance again on the sit-bones, extend arms and legs out into a V-sit (see fig. 3.02), then back to a tuck. Rinse and repeat. If balancing on the sit-bones is too challenging, place your feet on the floor to steady yourself as you roll up.

Figure **3.01**

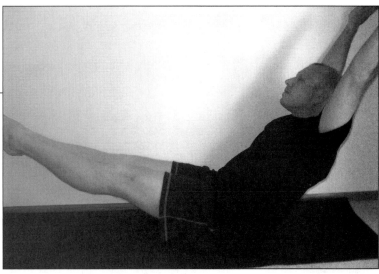

Figure 3.02

Pike: Pike position, holding imaginary caterpillars in the hands, lightly smack the sides of the thighs from the hips down, without smashing your caterpillars (see fig. 3.03). Lean over straight legs, extending as far as possible. Roll back into a plow, (fig. 3.04) then return and extend farther. Then roll back into a candlestick (shooting your legs straight up to the sky, body straight, hands either holding up your hips or flat on the floor), and again return and extend over your piked legs even farther.

Figure **3.03**

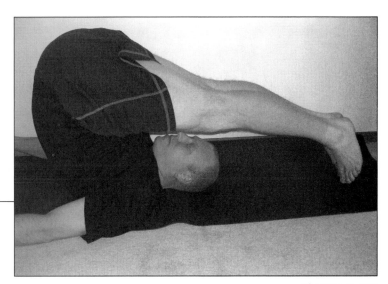

Figure **3.04**

Straddle: Straddle position, be sure the knees are pointed up toward the ceiling at all times (fig. 3.05). Lean over one leg, and the other, then the middle. Be sure movements are sustained and held. For straddle improvement, straddle up against a wall and ease your way wider gently and by small degrees.[2] Or use one of those creepy leg-widener devices if desired.

Stretching Positions #2

Hundreds and Hips: Lying on the back, lift the feet with bent knees, thighs perpendicular to the floor. Flex the hip joints by

Figure **3.05**

Figure **3.06**

switching the knees, one on top of the other, in an open-close motion of the hips. Then, freeze and lift the shoulders and head to look at the knees. Extend the arms straight out and slap the air shallowly as though there is a water surface there. (See fig. 3.06.) Breathe in for five counts and out for five counts; repeat one hundred times.

Figure 3.07

Downward Dog and Upward Cat: On hands and feet, sink the back between the shoulders, heels pushing down and head dangling (see fig. 3.07). This can be done with one foot hooked over the other

Achilles for more stretch, or put one foot between the hands and rise for a deep lunge. Bring knees back down to the floor and flatten the back. Arch spine up and down like a cat, then sink the knees with butt in the air for another version of the cat. (See figures 3.08 through 3.11.)

Figure **3.08**

Figure **3.09**

Figure **3.10**

Figure **3.11**

Boats and Bridges: Lying flat on the stomach, arch spine so the hands and feet are raised. Rock back and forth on the belly, keeping the arch (see fig. 3.12). Lying on the back, tighten the butt and belly to make a hollow. Rock back and forth on the spine, keeping your hollow tight (see fig. 3.13). Yoga Bridge: Lie on back, lift pelvis to the sky, flatten hands at the sides (see

Figure **3.12**

Figure **3.13**

Figure **3.14**

Figure **3.15**

fig. 3.14). Gymnastics Bridge: Lie on back, place hands flat on floor by the ears, press with hands and feet till belly hits the ceiling (see fig. 3.15). Do not come down on the head, or let go hands with head on the floor. Nasty neck injuries can result. For added torture, do the Gymnastics Bridge as push-ups.

Warm-Ups

These exercises get the blood pumping, and are good for a warm-up as opposed to the more cooling-down or slow limbering effects of the above stretches.

Swinging and Circling:[3] A "swing" is a 180-degree pendulum movement; a "swing" of the head only will start at one shoulder, then rock through chin-on-the-chest, then up to the other shoulder. A "circle" is a full 360-degree movement, so a circle of the head only will start at one shoulder, rock through center to the other shoulder, and back again. The rhythm starts with a set of just the head, then adds the shoulders, then the whole torso, then a set with bending knees, and finally a sidestep or twirl. For example, start by swinging the head to the left, then to the right, then in a full circle to the left, then to the right again. With each repetition of the pattern, let the rhythm engage more and more of the body. This exercise gets the blood flowing and the heart going, and sets the breath in tune with the swooping movement. Use music or merely the chant, "Swing . . . swing . . . c-i-r-c-l-e . . . swing." Don't fall! Be sure the body is soft when swooping, or tight muscles may strain.

Bridge Tag: The rules: One person is "it," randomly chosen by teacher or director. Anyone tagged must do a bridge, and must hold the bridge until someone else crawls under her (see fig.3.16). "It" changes randomly, by choice of the teacher or director. Substitute Downward Dog for bridges for the less skilled (see fig. 3.17).

Figure **3.16**

It *Is* as Easy as Falling off a Log

The main focus of taihenjutsu is the movement of the body as it pertains to falling and rolling. The following system of rolls and falls for all directions is a combination of universal stage combat techniques and martial arts techniques, both

Figure **3.17**

of which ensure that actors sustain no injuries when lowering their bodies to the ground. However, don't expect the falls and rolls to feel like a soft foam pit—these forms are good for realism and to keep actors from major injury, but stages are made of hard wood, so be very careful when starting out. If gymnastics or martial arts mats are available for beginning practice, they are highly recommended before moving falls and rolls to a harder surface.

Rolls

When learning rolls for the stage, be sure to go slowly at first, lowering your weight before you roll. Once you learn how to roll, practice with different distances. Make your rolls travel a long way, or not at all. Get rolling of all kinds under control, so you can safely direct rolls anywhere—you should know where you're going to end up and mean to end up there. These rolls can also be practiced from the knees or sitting as well as standing, or from one to the other. Always be careful of your bones when rolling, especially the spine and neck—a good exercise to practice non-bruising rolls is to try to keep rolls as quiet as possible. The more thumps and clunks, the more bones are hitting the floor!

Forward Somersault: Place your hands on the floor, look at your belly button, roll straight over your head—you should feel the floor touch all along your spine but not your head. Reach forward with your hands to get up (you shouldn't push down with your hands on the floor to get up—it's all in the abs!), end up standing. *Safety Tip*: Make sure you tuck your head way under—don't pile-drive it into the floor. Chin to your chest!

Forward Shoulder Roll: Place your hands in a "T" shape on the floor (see fig. 3.18).

Roll over the top-hand shoulder, and end up either kneeling or standing. The floor will touch your back at a diagonal, instead of straight over your spine, as in the somersault. This is a martial arts style of forward roll, done this way to save the back from inordinate strain. *Safety Tip*: Stop, Drop, and Roll—lower your weight as close to the floor as you can before you roll. Air-break falls and dive rolls are difficult and dangerous, and should not be practiced at all until the basic rolls are mastered and professional supervision is at hand.

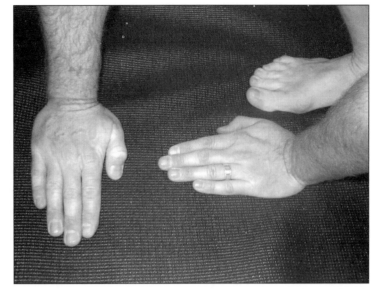

Figure 3.18

Backward Somersault:[4] Hold your hands by your ears as though you have pizzas ready to serve. Squat as low as you can and roll back straight down your back, all the way over your head. Smash your "pizzas" on the floor to aid in clearing your head. To get up, place your feet on the floor first, not your knees. *Safety Tip*: Chin to your chest, and use your momentum. If you stop after you sit, you'll never make it over.

Backward Shoulder Roll: Unlike the somersault, this roll can be started by sitting or kneeling without messing up the momentum needed to get over. Look over one shoulder, and roll over the opposite one. As in the forward shoulder roll, the floor will touch your back at a diagonal, and your head will be out of the way of the roll. End up kneeling or standing.

Actually, I recommend always using the shoulder rolls for stage, unless there is a particular reason why a somersault would work better for the scene. Why? Two big reasons: First, because the shoulder rolls cause much less strain on the spine and skull. Second, the shoulder rolls are much easier to do, especially the backward one—this makes them look less gymnastics-y and more natural, which is essential for most scenes where rolls are needed.

Sideways Roll: This is simply a barrel roll across the middle of the back. Practice from the martial arts position *hira no kamae* (see fig. 2.04, in chapter 2), step sideways, and roll sideways back up to your feet. A good way to keep your rolls on target (and your head from hitting the ground) is to have a partner stand in front of you and hold up a certain number of fingers as you roll. See if you can relay how many fingers were up when you've come up out of your roll.

Practice working this up to standing gradually: Begin with actors lying on backs, rocking back and forth from side to side. Then raise this same side-to-side rolling to the knees—see if you can start on knees, roll sideways, and end up on knees. Once you've worked the roll from these lower levels, try dropping into the roll from a standing position.

Falls

Falls are extremely important in stage combat—they pop up everywhere, both comedic pratfalls and realistic dramatic falls. To fall down onstage is also extremely dangerous, especially when the action is repeated every night for a long run. It is much more likely that an actor will be asked to do a fall onstage than a roll.

No actor should ever actually fall onstage. In other words, an actor's weight should always be under her control. During any of these falls, you should be able to stop the action and reverse it at any time. If you can't do this, then you're really falling, which isn't stage combat, it's . . . well, really falling. But even the best techniques can cause a little strain and pain, especially if, like most normal people, you avoid falling down as much as possible in day-to-day life. There are ways to condition and warm up a body to get it ready for a day of learning falls. Here are a few good exercises to do pre-falling:

Pliés: Your basic knee-bends. You can do these in ballet positions, or with feet parallel. In any case, remember to bend your knees over your feet; don't twist or torque as you bend, or you'll damage your joints badly. Be sure your back remains straight as well: Don't slouch and don't stick your butt out, or you'll damage your back. Imagine you're a carousel horse, with a pole going through your torso. You can move up and down on the pole, but your spine shouldn't bend, just your knees.

Lunges: Stage falls often require a deep lunge in order to lower the body's weight before touching the ground. Fencers practice lunges by placing a quarter under the big toe, then lunging forward while flicking the quarter as far as they can in front of them. The yoga position called Warrior Two involves rotating between a Downward Dog and a standing lunge, with arms straight out from the shoulders (See fig. 3.19).

Figure **3.19**

Downward Dogs and Push-Ups: These are good for balancing your center of gravity, taking weight onto the hands, and keeping a tight body position. Downward Dogs are also especially good for stretching out the calves, hamstrings and Achilles tendon area. Remember, a plank position (your push-up starting position) is flat-bodied, your back parallel to the floor, like fig. 3.20. The Downward Dog is an inverted V with your butt up to the sky, like fig. 3.07.

Figure **3.20**

Forward Fall: There are three basic steps to an effective, safe forward fall:

1. Deep lunge: Get your center as close to the ground as you can. Your large forward step should be slightly off-center, so as to have room for your body (see fig. 3.21).

2. Place your hands down onto the floor. Do not jam them or fall on them. Remember, you should be able to stop here and go backward (see fig. 3.22).

3. Lower yourself down to the floor, just like a push-up. You'll end up either on your stomach or your side (see fig. 3.23).

Safety Tip: Do this slowly several times before you bring it up to realistic speed. Practice freezing and reversing at different times during the fall to make sure you have full control of your weight at all times.

Partnered Exercise: For a safe push, see chapter 4. Combine a push with the forward fall: One partner stands behind the other and places her hands on her partner's shoulder blade. The falling partner isolates the shoulder back and then forward into this forward fall (see the *isolation exercises* in Chapter 4 for more information). You can then add a head slam (again, see chapter 4) to the scene once the falling partner has fallen.

A note regarding martial arts break falls: Anyone who knows something about the martial arts will know that a forward break fall takes the body's weight on the forearms (thus saving the wrists from nasty spiral fractures), with a satisfying *slap!* sound. This is a technically safe fall, if learned and practiced correctly. However, it is my opinion that if you actually fall (even in a professional break fall) onstage, you're asking for trouble. There are so many things that can happen even to a planned,

Figure **3.21**

Figure **3.22**

Figure **3.23**

professional fall: What if the wineglass that broke in the last scene wasn't cleaned up quite well enough? What if there's a rogue wood-screw loose in the floor? What if there's old electric tape that sticks to your shoe and trips you? The stage is rife with variables, seen and unseen, and is much, much more dangerous than a martial arts or dance studio. An actor should have utter control of her locomotion at all times; that way, if she notices something's not right, she can stop the "fall," save herself an injury, and maybe even save the scene.

Backward Fall: There are three basic steps to a backward fall as well:

Figure **3.24**

Figure **3.25**

1. Squat (see figures 3.24 and 3.25).

2. Sit (see fig. 3.26).

3. Lie down (see fig. 3.27).

Figure **3.26**

Figure **3.27**

That's it. You can shoot one foot forward in a slipped-on-a-banana-peel effect or merely squat—just make sure you lower your weight before you sit, or you could bruise a tailbone. *Safety Tip*: Don't let your head flop, or you could end up with whiplash or a floor-conked head. If you need to end up flat on the floor (see fig. 3.27), just be sure your head hitting the floor is not at speed—fall, then place the head down gently after all momentum is over. Special effects note: A real martial arts backward break fall smacks the hands on the floor. This can make a great sound onstage, but do be careful if you choose to do this—smacking your hands on a hard floor can sting mightily, even bruise.

Sideways Fall: This fall works the same as the backward fall, except banana-peel your leg to the side instead of forward. Watch that you don't catch your weight on your hip or wrists. Land on your meaty parts (thigh, butt) and be sure you can stop the fall at any time.

The Swoon: Stand with one foot slightly in front of the other. Pivot on your toes so that you are now facing sideways with crossed legs. Place your meaty bits on the floor in this order: butt, trapezius, tricep. Don't catch yourself on your wrist. Don't knock your elbows. Don't let your head flop. (See fig. 3.28.)

Figure **3.28**

The Captain Kirk: Wear knee pads if at all possible for this one. Many instructors teach this as a safe stage fall, but I'm personally

Figure **3.29**

Figure **3.30**

Figure **3.31**

Figure **3.32**

uncomfortable with anything so involved with my knees and the hard ground meeting. Anyway, be sure to practice this one ridiculously slowly for a very long time before bringing it up to speed. It goes as follows:

1. The brain-eating bug enters your ear (see fig. 3.29).[5]

2. Squat all the way down onto your hams (see fig. 3.30).

3. Place (*softly!*) one knee, then the other on the floor (see fig. 3.31).

4. Call for Dr. Bones (see fig. 3.32).

Safety Tip: If an actor's knees go *kerthunk* onstage, the audience will not hear a word of his brilliant Shakespearean soliloquy. Instead, they'll wince and moan. Then they'll wonder if he's okay for the rest of the scene or until he gets up, whichever comes first. Maybe not even then. *Another Safety Tip*: There is nothing wrong with requesting that knee and elbow pads be included in a costume. Unless the costume is lingerie or something equally revealing, most pads can be concealed easily under most costumes. Why push it?

Jumping and Leaping

A *jump* takes off from two feet and lands on two feet. A *leap* takes off from one foot and lands on the opposite foot (like a giant step in the air). A *hop* takes off from one foot and lands on the same foot.

Are you with me so far? Good.

Now then: An *assemblé* takes off from one foot and lands on two feet. A *sissone* takes off from two feet and (you guessed it) lands on one foot. Got it? Go practice. If you get confused, ask your friendly neighborhood ballet professional, or log on to *www.abt.org*.[6]

When practicing your jumps of all kinds, try to make your landings as silent as possible. Bend your knees—use all the natural shock absorbers in the legs to eliminate harsh, thumping landings. *Safety Tip*: Gymnasts scoop their arms straight up above their heads when they jump. It lifts them higher into the air and also lowers air resistance when doing turning jumps.

It's a good idea to warm up and do some conditioning before getting into lots of jumping. Jumping jacks are great as a preliminary, to start jumping before you start jumping! I suggest jumping jacks every morning for a healthy heart and big breaths. It's nearly as good a wake-up call as coffee. Nearly. Also, look at chapter 2 for any array of warm-ups you like: pliés, the different sitting positions (tuck, straddle, and pike), and Swinging and Circling are all good ones for jumping.

Jumping Attention Exercise: For your stretches on a jump-practice day, do the tuck, straddle, and pike positions on the floor and stretch in those positions. They'll help with leg and spine flexibility, and will get your body into the positions even before you try them in a jump. Then have one person randomly call out the jump variations below and the rest of the group try to match the call together.

Tuck: A tuck jump is a jump with the knees pulled up to the chest. Legs should straighten before landing a tuck jump, or you'll land crouched or fall over.

Straddle: A jump with legs straight, apart, and forward, like a straddle-sit in the air. Be sure to land with feet together, or knee injuries can occur.

Pike: A jump with legs straight, together, and forward. Reach your hands toward your feet. Be sure to bring your feet back under yourself quickly, or you'll land crooked and hurt your knees or back.

Half-Turn and Full Turn: A half-turn is a straight jump that turns 180 degrees. Take off facing the front, and land facing the back wall. A full turn is a 360-degree jumping turn. Take off facing front, turn all the way around, and land facing front again. Lifting your arms above your head like a gymnast is especially useful for full turns.

Spotting in Turns: Pick something at eye level to look at. Turn around slowly until you can't look at it anymore, then whip your head around as fast as you can to spot it again. Practice spotting in slow turns first, then gradually speed up until you're spotting in your jumping turns. Spotting helps with balance and dizziness in turns. Just watch a ballet dancer pirouette a million times in a row—you can see her head whipping around each time to spot.

Acrobatics and an Opinionated Note Regarding Trampolines

Stage combat is about safety first. Ask stage fight professionals whether they would sacrifice the realism of a scene in order to stay safe, and the answer will be a resounding "yes." If a technique gets messed up, if an actor suddenly forgets choreography in the middle of a scene, the most important thing to do is to stop. Sure, the scene may be ruined, the character broken, but better to break character than to break bones.

Trampolines have found their way into many backyards all over America; in the minds of many unassuming parents, they are just expensive toys. But owning a trampoline is about as dangerous as owning a sword, or even a gun (more so, since most people would never allow a child to play with an obvious weapon). Trampolines propel one very high. Whenever one's feet leave the ground, the safety rules change, let alone when you leave the ground as high as a trampoline can get you. Just a "normal" jump that lands slightly off-center can either toss one off the trampoline or jam one's back. Countless times as a gymnastics instructor I heard this phrase uttered by seven- to ten-year-olds: "But I already know how to do a flip—I do it at home on my trampoline all the time." If one is upside down, things get even more dangerous. What happens when one lands on the back of the neck? Paralysis. Yes, Virginia, even on a trampoline.

My point? When jumping, rolling, or going upside down, *be careful*! Start slow and basic, and spot your friends. Most of all, do these techniques *correctly*—there is no such thing as "It's okay, it didn't hurt." If you're doing it unsafely, it will hurt eventually and you'll regret it. Again, don't be tough; be right.

Conditioning is super-important even for the following simple acrobatics skills, since going upside down onto one's hands takes quite a toll on those poor little wrist bones. The following exercises are good wrist stretches for anytime, but especially for limbering up the wrists before practicing the basic acrobatics below. Wristbands are good for solidity as well—they don't actually hold your wrists together, but are good reminders of what proper alignment should be (and they soak up sweat to boot).

Roller Coaster: Clasp your hands together in front of you, then roll both arms in a wave motion, in both directions (see fig. 3.33). Nostalgic for break-dancing?

Washing Machine: Clasp your hands together in front of you, then twist your wrists back and forth. Be gentle (see fig. 3.34).

Figure **3.33**

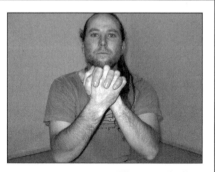

Figure **3.34**

Ninja IQ Test #1: Hold your hand out straight as if about to shake hands. Then, flip your hand over so that your thumb is pointing downward (see fig. 3.35). Grasp it with your free hand, and fold wrist, bringing it in to your sternum.

Figure **3.35**

Figure **3.36**

Your arm should have a "Z"-like shape. For more stretch, push your pinky up toward the sky (see fig. 3.36). For less stretch, ease up on the folded wrist.

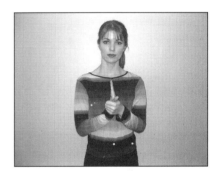

Figure **3.37**

Ninja IQ Test #2: Hold your hand upright, with straight fingers pointing straight up at the sky. Reach all the way around with your other hand and grasp your thumb, pulling the hand all the way around as far as it comfortably goes, spiral twisting your wrist. For more stretch, bring the twisted hand close and down to your sternum (see fig. 3.37). For less stretch, ease up on the twisted wrist.

Seals: Lie down flat on the floor, face down. Lift your torso up by pushing down on the floor with your palms, gripping with your fingertips. Now you're in a *cobra* (see fig. 3.38). Then, turn your hands out, pointing your fingertips to each side. Rock gently side to side, letting your shifting weight massage your wrists.

Figure **3.38**

Shake It Off: Sit comfortably and shake your hands out, in all directions. Think of it as flinging water drops off your hands.

Basic Acrobatics

Acrobatics will rarely be needed in a theatrical production. The following basics are good to practice for movement and spatial awareness, and the special mobility involved in getting yourself upside down, supported on your hands instead of your overused feet. For exhibition-type shows that are more about skill display than story, these flashier movements can be useful for choreography. But do be sure in such cases to use movement professionals, not just this manual, for guidance and safety. Sticking with basic falls and rolls not only is safest, but also reads most effectively to an audience. Though you may be excited to use the high school gymnast you just cast, stop and think: What can an audience clearly follow onstage? Are the actors' lines speakable and audible within the physicality? You'll find that when you're linking techniques together for full fight choreography, keeping it simple is best. Just be sure the taihenjutsu and other techniques you use match the characters and scene involved. Who is going to cartwheel in a fight scene? Maybe an over-the-top ninja character, but not Hamlet.

Headstand: Always make sure your neck is in alignment when you're stacking your body weight on top of it. For a headstand, imagine (or draw) a triangle on the floor, with your head as the apex and your hands shoulder-width apart. Start with a *tripod*: that is, move your knees slowly toward yourself until you can place your knees on your elbows (see fig. 3.39). Only when this feels secure should you lift your feet into the air. When your tripod feels solid, slowly straighten your legs and body into a headstand (see fig. 3.40). *Safety Tip:* It's fine to practice this against a wall for balance, but be careful that you don't arch in order to meet the wall. Make

Figure **3.39**

sure your spine is in alignment over your head.

Inversion: An inversion is a brief weight transfer: Just put your hands down and let them take your weight for a moment, then come back down. This is not a handstand, so there's no need to kick up high or hold it for any length of time.

Figure **3.40**

Handstand: Place your hands shoulder-width apart on the floor. Be sure your shoulders are over your hands. Shift one foot as close to your hands as you can get it, and straighten the other leg toward the sky. Do small *grasshopper kicks* to get the feel of it: Keep your leg straight, and keep your hands glued to the floor (see fig. 3.41). The idea is to eventually stack your feet over your hips over your shoulders

Figure 3.41

over your hands. Once you've practiced enough grasshopper kicks to make you turn blue, you can begin to meet your feet in the air (see fig. 3.42). Be sure to land on the same foot you took off from. *Safety Tip:* If you kick up too hard and are tipping over, either twist your body to land on your feet, or tuck your head and forward-roll out of it.

Never bridge out of a handstand or fall on your back. A variation on entering a handstand is to begin with your back against a wall. Bend over so that your butt is on the wall and your hands are touching the floor. Walk your feet up the wall as far as they will go. Watch your back to make sure it doesn't sink into overarching. Once your strength builds up through practice, walk your hands back to the wall after you're upside down.

Figure 3.42

Cartwheel: Reach all the way over your head with both hands. Place one hand, then the other, on the floor, then land one foot, then the other. If you begin facing one wall, you should end up facing the same wall; this involves a pivot that can be tricky to get right. Start with baby ones, then kick up higher and higher until you end up looking like the spokes of a wheel. A *Front-to-Back Cartwheel* is the same (hand-hand-foot-foot), except that you begin facing forward and end up facing the direction from which you came (see fig. 3.43).

Handsprings: You don't need these—they're too dangerous. I'll teach them to you in a class if you want, but you don't need them for any basic stage combat. Seriously. Go practice your cartwheels.

Figure 3.43

Okay, okay, here are the basics. *Please* do these with a spotter! And mats!! A *forward handspring* is similar to a forward roll, except that instead of curving your spine and rolling over your back, you keep looking at your hands and push off the floor hard with your shoulders. A strong handspring uses the shoulders to push, not a bending of the elbows. Land on your feet. A *backward handspring* begins by standing with knees bent, arms straight and forward (gymnasts call this a "stop" or "stick" position). Jump back and up, springing off your hands and landing on your feet. Again, push with the big shoulder muscles, not the small arm muscles. Handsprings are an advanced skill; there should be no reason to attempt these techniques without professional help. Large octagon-shaped mats or giant inflatable exercise balls are good for preliminary handspring practice: Arch either forward or backward over the mat or ball, and rock back and forth between hands and feet. Learning handsprings on a trampoline is also a good set of "training wheels" for those interested in adding handsprings to their future movement arsenal. Cartwheels are good practice as well.

Conclusion: Movement Game

Walk, Double-Time, Collapse:[7] This exercise is for a group, large or small. Everyone begins by taking a walk around the space. Practice seamlessly dropping to the floor and holding a shape there. Then, use a drumbeat or other pulse to walk to, double-time (run) to, and pepper this with falls (fig. 3.44). So each person in the group can choose to walk, run, fall, and get up right away, or fall and hold a shape at any time. The result is a dynamic improvisatory dance with heightened spatial awareness for each of the dancers. It's also a good way to get used to falling on a hard dance floor or stage floor without making huge clunking noises and incurring bumps and bruises. Adapt this game to include any of the taihenjutsu techniques in a mix for practice, vocabulary response, quick thinking, and quick moving.

Figure 3.44

---

[1]   All stretching exercises are from the author's personal experience in dance, Pilates, gymnastics, aerial dance, acting prep, yoga, and martial arts classes, both taken and taught.

[2]   My dancer mom used to talk on the phone while straddling against the wall. Her middle-aged straddle is still spectacularly limber (no matter what she says).

3   Speaking of dancer mom . . . Zukowski, Ginger. *On the Move.* SIU Press, 1990.

4   Look at Lessac's *Body Wisdom* for the sections on the body-as-sphere for
      more exercises to get into rolls. It's nice for the nervous or unskilled.

5   I know, I know, it was Chekhov, not Kirk, who had the bug in the ear.

6   American Ballet Theatre, *Ballet Dictionary,*
      www.abt.org/education/dictionary/index.html.

7   Morgenroth, *Dance Improvisations*, 38.

Chapter Four

Unarmed Combat

The victim is always in control. The victim is always in control. The victim is always in control. . . .[1]

Let this be the mantra for any partnered stage combat technique either learned or taught. Chant it together as a vocal warm-up before each rehearsal. Write it over and over again in your journal as you process the techniques. If you remember this mantra constantly, you are already halfway to ultimate safety.

Part of keeping the victim in control is using proper cues and proper distancing between partners as they practice. *Eye contact* is an essential cue for all of the following techniques in all of the following chapters, and there will be a set place within each move for partners to "check in" with each other: Are they on the same page? Have they forgotten anything? Does the receiving actor know a very dangerous fake punch is coming in, and will he react with proper timing and safety? Use the *isolation exercises* toward the end of this chapter every day when practicing stage combat to get partners in sync with each other and to get ready to use movement to tell the audience a story.

Some Shakespeare buffs and Renaissance Faire folk will no doubt be whining by now, "But Jenn, when do we get to use our swords?" To them, I say: Easy there, my cousins. If you don't yet have the grasp of how two bodies look and feel in conflict, then no amount of sword-waving will give you a good-looking fight (and you remember what I've said about swords and safety). Unarmed fighting is the most versatile set of stage combat skills you can have when arranging your "bag of tricks" for any play. Not every theatrical production is Shakespeare, and not every Shakespeare is done with proper Renaissance attire and weaponry. The following unarmed techniques work as well in a Shakespearean tragedy as in a modern slapstick comedy or a kung fu film. Once you have the basic moves down unarmed, translating your combat understanding to any weapon at all will be a relatively simple matter.

Conditioning and Warm-Ups

Punching Bag: Well, why not? It's a good thing to know what actual contact feels like if one is going to fake it realistically. Especially for my female friends out there: I have witnessed too many strong women who get into a stage combat class and "punch like a girl," only because they haven't had any experience with this particular movement. Go punch a bag, a pillow, or a tree if you're feeling tough. It'll help your technique, and honestly, is quite therapeutic.[2]

Leg Swings and Helicopters: You can use a ballet barre or table to keep your balance at first, then attempt some leg swings without holding on! Keep your spine straight and your hips in line, and swing your leg up and back from the hip joint. If you find that your hips tilt, you're attempting to kick too high. You don't need to be a Rockette—just swing each leg naturally. It oils up your hip joints and helps your balance.

For *helicopters*, plant your feet and swing your arms from side to side, twisting each way. You can also do *arm circles*: Start with your arms straight out from your shoulders, circling your straight arms in tiny circles first, then widening and widening until you become the helicopter. Do forward and backward circles to loosen up the shoulder joints and get the blood flowing in the arms and hands.

Look! Elvis!: Get a stable stance (the martial arts "horse stance" is a good one; see fig. 4.01) and look up as far as your neck lets you. Then left, then right, then down, then up again. Practice your side-to-side looks sharply but carefully, as this movement will be repeated when you learn slaps and punches as the victim. Then, roll your neck in soft, complete circles. *Safety Note:* Many movement arts practitioners will squeal if head circles include circling back. There isn't any problem with moving your neck in a full circle, including back, as long as you are careful (as usual). When your neck circles back, don't let it flop and crunch those neck vertebrae—be sure you have your head slightly lifted, with some space back there as you circle. To get used to it, place the first two fingers of each hand behind your neck as you circle—that's the amount of space you're looking for.

Figure 4.01

Figure **4.02**

Mirrors: See chapter 3 for an introduction to mirrors. Emphasize partner connection when doing mirrors before practicing unarmed techniques: If partners have been mirrors to each other, they can more readily connect when it comes to isolation, eye contact, and safe distance later. Mirrors can help partners get used to each other's movement dynamic and body type, which can make for more seamless unarmed practice when moving together (almost like dance choreography) is necessary (see fig. 4.02).

Zap: This can be done in a full group, in small groups, or with partners. It's a simple theatre pep game: Shout *Zap!* while flinging your arms out toward another person. That person then takes that energy and *Zap!*s someone else. Start with arms, then use other parts and eventually the whole body to fling *Zap!*s at each other.

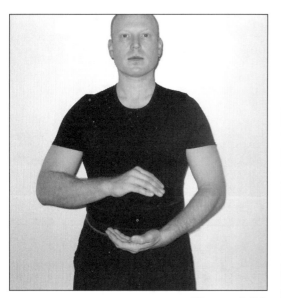

Figure 4.03

Tai Chi Ball: Rub your hands together vigorously until heat builds. Then, slowly separate the hands, palms always facing each other. Circle the palms as you slowly pull your hands apart farther and farther. The sensation should be akin to holding the two opposite ends of magnets near each other. Feel the palpable magnetic repelling force, and see how wide apart your hands can be while still feeling this sensation. Try it with a partner. How big can the tai chi ball get before you lose the sensation? (See fig. 4.03.)

Unarmed Distancing

Now that we've gotten into illusions of violence, the importance of *distancing* is even more important with all the techniques to follow. Proper distance can be the difference between major injury and safety, between the ridiculously fake and a technique so real, the audience will think it has actually happened. Go back and read the unlucky thirteen things that can happen to you when you land a slap, and then practice the following distancing exercises.

In order to find proper safe distance for unarmed combat, one partner makes the "hang loose" sign (a fist with thumb and pinky finger extended) with the hand, then places the thumb in the middle of the chest. The other partner extends her arm as far as it goes until it meets the extended pinky of the other partner (see fig. 4.04). This is *proper distance* for both unarmed stage combat and that with weapons. It is close enough that the illusion of contact is real for the audience, yet the essential space the "hang loose" gives you is the safety space. If one partner throws a punch (try it) and the other partner forgets he was going to and doesn't move, the punch sails harmlessly by. Now that you have this magic formula, practice moving into and out of proper distance.

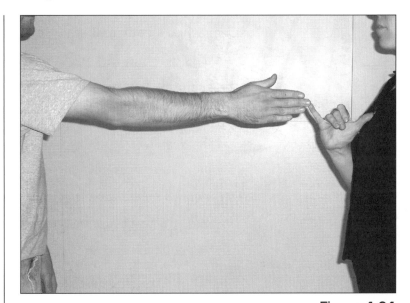

Figure 4.04

Take a walk around the room after establishing partners beforehand. Have fun with low-, middle-, and high-level movements and different speeds of movement around the room, and be sure that partners don't stay stuck together. Then, on a count or drumbeat of three, find your partner and freeze in proper distance. Once you've frozen, test your accuracy by doing the "hang loose" test. Are you too close? Too far away? Just right? Try again, experimenting with different counts to find each other. The Eight-Count exercise from chapter 3 modifies very well into this exercise, or can be done as a warm-up.

Body Planes and Audience Perspective

Most safe stage combat techniques keep the attack away from the victim's body at all times, using intention, distancing, and knowing when it's appropriate to cross the planes of the partner's body and when it's too dangerous. For example, partners will find that with the sword techniques, the point of the sword never crosses the center plane of the face. For slaps and punches, audience perspective is a useful tool for keeping energy flung past a partner's body and not into it. In the first slap technique, for example, the attacker's hand flings energy past the victim's head, looking for all the world like contact has been made, whereas in reality there are several inches between the victim's face and the attacker's hand, and no inward intention toward the face at all. Another good mantra to remember is: Send the energy *out*, not *in*.

Remember: The victim is in control. A mediocre slap technique with a good reaction reads well to an audience. An elaborate, silent slap with no "real" sound, actor placement, and pain reaction doesn't look good, no matter how technically correct the actors are. The idea is to tell the story of the action to the audience. An audience experiences combat illusions as part of the story. Windup, slap sound, reaction of pain: That's how an audience understands an act of violence has happened. Think of stage combat as a physical continuation of a scene's dialogue. An off technique will leave an audience confused: Did that guy get slapped in the neck? How come there was no sound when that chick got hit? What just happened?

And Speaking of Sound: It's Knap-Time!

Good sounds are essential to the realism of a piece of combat. I'm not talking witty banter between moves (like the main sword-fighting scene in *The Princess Bride*), but the real sounds that physical contact makes, and the real effort-grunts that people make when beating each other up. Make sure that you are grunting always with effort and pain, and not in too regular a rhythm. It keeps you breathing and sounds realistic.

The term "knap" refers to the sound one body part makes when hitting another. Knaps can be done by the attacker, the victim, both together, or (rarely) by a third party. Sometimes the knap is light contact (such as in the stomach punch); sometimes it's a setup and hidden artificial sound.

Clap Knap: Hold one hand relaxed at the sternum. Bring the other hand up against it to make a loud clap. This is good for slaps, as the aftermath of the clap motion can be disguised as a victim reaction of holding the slapped face.

Chest Knap: This is a good sound for punches. Practice thumping yourself on the upper pectoral muscle (not the collarbone, not the breast!) with an open hand. When you are the attacker for punch techniques, you can effectively mask this knap inside the punching arm.

Contact Knaps: These are techniques that use actual contact as the sound for the technique. The *stomach punch* is the easiest example of the contact knap: It sounds way more painful than it really is! (See fig. 4.22.) As long as you use a hollow, loose fist, the punch will snap off the victim's stomach with a strong noise and no injury to the victim. The safe area is right on the biggest muscle—just below the belly button. Avoid the solar plexus (too high) or groin (too low).

Contact knaps also show up in the *face kick* and the *all-fours stomach kick*. Contact kicks? Whoa, isn't that dangerous? I'm not talking crazy talk. The key to contact in kicks is to touch with the top of the foot. Toes, a rigid foot, the blade of the foot (pinky-toe edge): These are all dangerous, but a floppy, loose ankle and flat top of the foot is about as safe as a loose fist. Make sure your *targets* are correct, too—nobody likes a kick in the solar plexus, loose-ankled or not.

The third type of contact knap is the shared knap of the *diagonal slap*, wherein the victim's hand is half the clap that the attacker launches (see fig. 4.10). The kneeling face kick actually works in a similar way. See the technique descriptions below for more details. Just keep in mind that contact knaps are loud and safe when the both actors are *relaxed*.

Voice "Knaps": Though not technically knaps, using a good grunt can mask a too-soft or nonexistent knap effectively. Try it in the knee-to-stomach technique: The victim's "ugh" is the only knap possible here, and the only knap needed.

Third-Party Knaps: The third-party knap is rarely used, and even more rarely done well. Think of it as having a foley artist for the stage. In cases wherein the audience is extremely close, extremely in the round, or extremely in some other situation when one of the above knaps can't possibly be masked, the contact sound for a bit of violence can be made by an "innocent bystander."[3] As long as the sound the third person makes is not calling attention to her but looks as though it is coming from the fighters, it can work. Timing is precise and essential for a third-party knap. Obviously, when working in film, most if not all of the combat sounds will be added later. Onstage, they must happen right with the movements.

Basic Unarmed Techniques

As you practice these, play with audience perspective: You'll notice some techniques work well in a variety of placements, and some work from one angle only. As your unarmed vocabulary comes more naturally, so too will smooth movement into and out of distance, and into and out of effective audience perspective. Show these techniques to each other and move the "audience" around: Some techniques will have only one bad angle, while some will look fantastically real when partners are three feet away from each other! Record your findings in your journal as part of your technique exploration.

Slaps

A slap is a strike with an open hand. The dynamic and style of a slap will vary depending on the dynamic and style of the characters using it. Slaps can range from the classic eighties-movie-girl-slaps-cad-boyfriend to a nasty backhand. As with all unarmed techniques, though, practice these first in a neutral style to get the mechanics down. Once you understand how the stage slap works, you can experiment with different styles.

Plain Ol' Slap: The attacker will wind up, keeping eye contact with the victim (see fig. 4.05). The attacker then shoots her open hand straight out, a couple inches away from the victim's same-side ear (see fig. 4.06 and 4.07). The victim reacts with a clap knap and straight face-turn, and the attacker draws her open hand back to her own opposite shoulder (see fig. 4.08).

Be careful that the attacker doesn't cross the plane of the victim's face when pulling her hand back. Also be careful that there's no hooking or leaning too much, or safe distance will get closed.

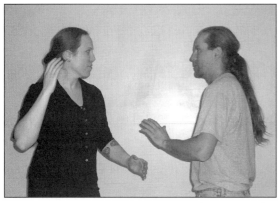

Figure **4.05**

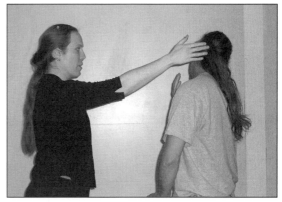

Figure **4.06**

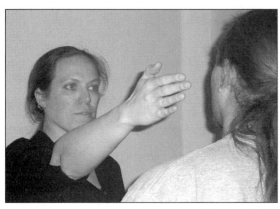

Figure **4.07**

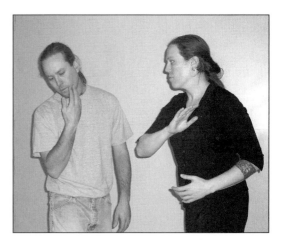

Figure **4.08**

When aiming the slap, imagine flicking energy straight *past* the victim's head. This will give realism to the slap and also keep you from turning your slap in toward the victim's face. Finally, be sure the slap is high enough, or you'll be showing the audience the infamous "neck slap," which doesn't look right at all.

Diagonal Slap: This slap only works with either the victim's or the attacker's back directly facing the audience. This slap goes from low to high with a shared knap. The victim sets his relaxed

Figure 4.09

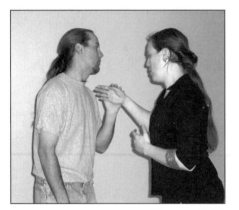

Figure 4.10

Figure 4.11

knap-hand in front of his sternum. The attacker winds up low, being sure to show the audience the slapping hand (see fig. 4.09). The attacker then claps the back of her hand against the palm of the victim's set knap-hand, following through the plane of the victim's face, through the whole diagonal (see fig. 4.10). The victim reacts at the correct angle (see fig. 411). Be sure you don't react with your hand too much, or the audience will wonder why you got slapped in the hand. Oh, and take your rings off!

Punches

A good-looking and safe stage combat fist is a slightly hollow, slightly loose fist. Imagine you are holding birds' eggs in your hands: Your fist must keep its shape or the eggs will fall to the ground, but you cannot squeeze your fists rigidly either because you'd crush the eggs.

A punch snaps back or follows through, depending on the type of punch it is. Avoid the habit of the "hanging fist." In other words, always snap your fist back or let it drift down after a follow-through. For some reason, punches tend to hang there like cartoons unless the attacker makes a concerted effort at following through.

Fist Terms: *Supinated* means palm-up, like a stereotypical karate punch (fig. 4.12). *Pronated* means palm-

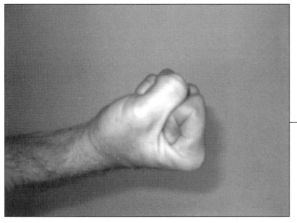

Figure 4.12

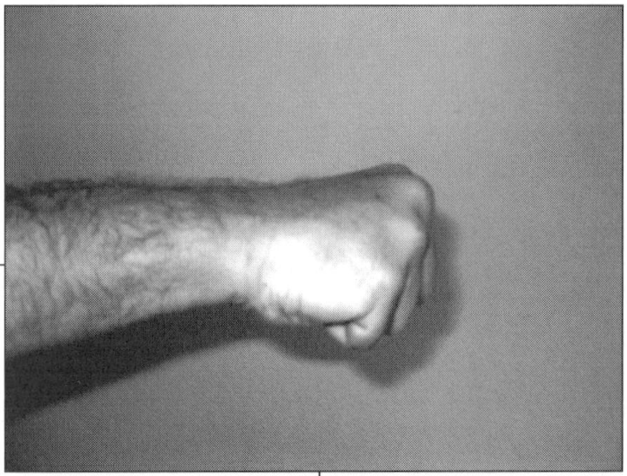

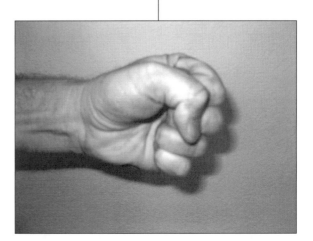

Figure 4.13

down, like a stereotypical Western punch (fig. 4.13). The *jab* is neither (some instructors call it *goofinated*): a fist with pinky side down, index-finger side up (fig. 4.14). Learn the following punches in their set position, then play around with pronation and supination after you've learned and are comfortable with the techniques.

Figure 4.14

Straight Punch: First, find proper distance. The victim's back should be to the audience, with the attacker facing him, or the other way around. Make *eye contact* as the attacker winds up.

The attacker should wind up with her forearm parallel to the ground and fist in line with the victim's nose (fig. 4.15). Remember, you are about a foot away from each other if you found proper distance—the audience angle flattens out the

Figure 4.15

perspective so it'll look like you've punched the victim's face when in fact you are pretty far apart. As the attacker winds up, she needs to check that the audience can see her fist—that the victim's face or body doesn't block her windup. The attacker then pivots feet first, with hips then shoulders following, and with the punching arm crossing just in front of her own face. Be sure the attacking arm ends up straight, then let it drift toward the floor for realism (see fig. 4.16). Practice without a knap first, then add a chest knap once you've got an idea of the timing with your partner.

A real punch like this would land directly on the victim's cheek. So the victim's reaction should be from that cheek, a

Figure 4.16

straight head snap sideways. The reaction shouldn't angle up or down too far unless the attacking partner has angled her punch that way. Practice this punch straight (parallel to the floor) until both partners are comfortable, then experiment with different angles: high to low, low to high. Make sure the victim really *snaps* his head with the reaction, as this adds to the realism.

Both partners: Once you become comfortable with the effects of this punch, play with different action/reaction pairings. See which pairings are comedic, realistic, just plain wrong; what happens when a small woman "lands" a small punch on a big man, and he flies across the room? What happens when he punches her back with his huge muscular arm and she barely moves her face from the "impact"? Notice the dynamic and speed of your partner and match your reaction for realism. Learn the difference between a realistic reaction and an outlandish one—both can be useful to you. Do this experiment with the basic slaps as well.

Figure **4.17**

Safety Tip: Experimentation is important for your deeper understanding of the dynamics of staged violence, but when you are learning this (and other punches) for the first time, practice in a neutral style and matching dynamic. Once the techniques are heavily rehearsed and second nature, then you can have more freedom for stretching them to suit your needs (see fig. 4.17).

Parrot Punch: This punch works best with the audience positioned on either side, not in front of or behind the combatants, as the space between fist and face will be apparent. But as always, experiment with perspective to truly experience the effects.

The attacker first imagines that the victim has a parrot sitting on his shoulder.[4] She'll make eye contact to be sure he's ready, then extend her fist in a jab position straight forward to punch that imaginary parrot, and snap back. Don't worry—the parrot can take it.[5] The key here is to keep the punch *straight*, so that she's punching air, which doesn't bleed, as opposed to her partner's face, which does. Imagining the parrot keeps the attacker from drifting in toward her partner's face or ear (see fig. 4.19). As partners learn this, they should practice silently for a while, then add a chest knap once they get the hang of it. Be sure in any case to *snap* the attacking fist back—it should look like the attacker punched something solid, not like he reached through the victim's face. For the same reason, be sure parrot punches don't show beyond the back of the victim's head. If his reaction is on time, it shouldn't be a problem.

The real punch is a jab smack in the middle of the nose. Gently push your nose straight back—see what happens to your head? Victim, keep this in mind as you react. For this technique, a head bobble after the initial head snap backward can be effective (see fig. 4.18).

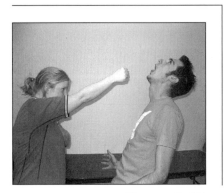

Figure **4.18**

Snake Punch: This is a useful punch when performing in the round or in small theatres, as it's closer than normal safe distance, and shows on both sides of the victim's face, leaving no bad angle. However, it is also an extremely dangerous punch for exactly the same reasons, so as you learn this one, be careful, and go slowly at first.

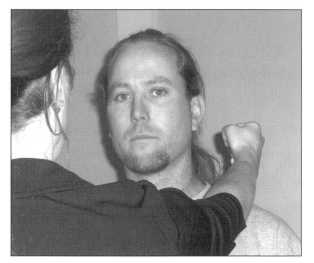

Figure 4.19

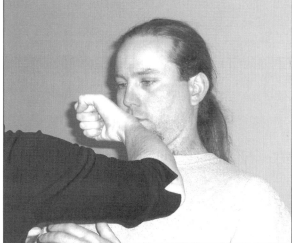

Figure 4.20

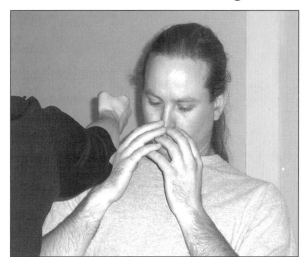

Figure 4.21

The attacker this time imagines *two* parrots, one on each of the victim's shoulders. She'll punch the first straight on, exactly like a normal parrot punch (see fig. 4.19), then carefully snake her fist around the victim's face (clearing his nose, please)(see fig. 4.20), and punch the other parrot (see fig. 4.21). What the snaking does is give the illusion of the fist meeting the face, with no bad angle for a masked amount of space. Obviously, this technique doesn't really look right until it's at full speed, but resist the impulse to speed it up too quickly at the expense of safety.

The victim's reaction should be the same as the reaction to the normal parrot punch, as the "real" version would be the same type of jab. When the audience is in the round, it's often easier to mask a clap knap done by the victim as opposed to the attacker, especially with this punch, but experiment and see for yourself what works for your setup.[6]

Note: The above three punches can be done with a sword as well. See chapter 6 for ways to adapt these unarmed techniques for armed fights.

Variation: For a *cross punch*, set up and find distance the same way you would for the regular parrot punch, wind up, and punch the opposite parrot. So instead of actually punching both parrots, like in the Snake Punch, you're cutting a diagonal line directly to the second parrot—no snaking motion involved. If you're tempted to try the Snake Punch when setting a fight, try the Cross Punch first—if it's effectively masked, it's a safer alternative, it's in safe distance, and it still has a similar effect as far as audience view plane, though it isn't a jab like the snake punch.

Stomach Punch: Why stick to only punching the victim's face? Stomachs are just as punchable, and they provide their own knaps!

With a hollow fist,[7] the attacker lightly snap-punches the victim's belly. No, really, it's okay, go ahead. Now try moderate contact. Nice sound, huh? Just be sure to hit with the flat of the fingers (no sharp knuckles) and be sure your target is just below his belly button (fig. 4.22). Too low and you're punching his groin (ouch), too high and you're punching his solar plexus, which can actually knock him out if you're hitting hard enough. But as long as you're careful, this contact is safe. No knap is needed besides the sound of the contact (and your victim's brilliant acting, of course). If the victim is uncomfortable with the contact or has an especially sensitive stomach, this punch can be done with no contact at all—the knap turns into the victim's vocal and physical reaction only.

Figure **4.22**

The victim should practice curling around the contact area, firming the belly muscles (have you done your Pilates today?), and letting out a "hup" or other realistic gruntlike sound. When one is punched in the stomach for real, one's breath gets knocked out.

Kicks

Almost all of the fundamental stage kicks described below use contact. Central to safe kick contact is making sure the kicker has a loose ankle and that contact is made with the top of the foot, not the toes, not the blade of the foot (the pinky-toe edge), not the heel. Also important to remember is the proper *target* for each technique. Aiming just a bit too high or too low can mean at least pain, at most injury, to the victim. A conditioning suggestion for kicks is to practice lunges, pliés, straddles, splits, and leg swings before working on kicks for any length of time. Tai chi is also good—anything to lubricate and stretch the hip joints, knees, and leg muscles. See the splits drill below for good kick conditioning.

Figure 4.23

Figure 4.24

Figure 4.25

Splits Drill: Begin on the knees, thighs perpendicular to the floor. Extend one leg out straight forward. Check alignment: Both hips should be pointed forward, and the extended toe should be in line with the knee in line with the hip. Sit back a little and bend over the extended knee (kiss your knee if you can) (fig. 4.23). Then straighten and bend the extended knee so that it is at a 90-degree angle. Straighten the back leg (fig. 4.24). If you're feeling like a yoga-monster, lift your arms to the sky and look up at the ceiling. Check your hips—are they still pointed forward? Straighten the front leg again and kiss your knee a second time. Now, straighten both legs. Sink as far as possible while keeping both legs straight and both hips forward (fig. 4.25). Rinse and repeat (on the other side). Do this every day, and eventually you'll be sitting on the floor in your split. No, really. Every day. Yes, it'll take a long time, depending on your age and innate flexibility—but never say never!

Knee to Stomach: Well, it *looks* like a knee to the stomach, but it's actually the top of the thigh to the stomach. Make eye contact first, and get ready to make some air-knocked-out and attacker noise, as this technique has no knap to speak of. The attacker places her hands on the victim's shoulders and makes eye contact for a cue. Then she tilts her hips so that the top of her thigh is in line with the victim's belly. She *does not* pull down on his shoulders to make contact—it's a light placement of the thigh on his belly, and let him do the hunching over.

The victim places his hands on the attacker's incoming thigh, then guides it to his belly (not too low, not too high), and hunches over the attacking leg, making the "hoo" sound of air getting knocked out (we did this sound in the stomach-punch technique). Remember, the victim is in control! This can also be done without holding the attacker's leg; just be sure both partners don't clonk heads or arms don't get in the way of incoming knees (see fig. 4.26).

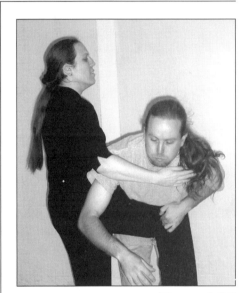

Figure 4.26

All Fours Stomach Kick: It's easy to skip the eye-contact moment in this technique, as the attacker is standing and the victim is on all fours. *Don't forget!* If the victim isn't ready, he can really get clocked badly on the ribs or solar plexus.

The attacker first must make sure there are no metal ornaments or the like in her shoelaces. Practice slowly by bringing the top of the foot smoothly and loosely up, lightly smacking the victim's stomach safely and softly low and to the side. It is in actuality more of a side kick than a stomach kick, though the audience is none the wiser. Instead of a snap-back like the stomach punch, the attacker will allow her foot to follow through the plane of the victim's body for realism. Think of it more as drawing the foot up than actually kicking very far out. The attacker's leg should never be fully extended in this technique. Shake out and loosen the ankles before practice to ensure that the foot won't go rigid and catch the victim with a sharp toe.

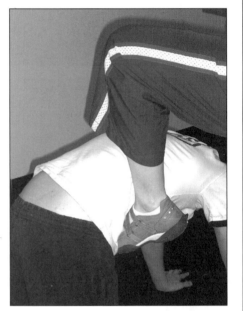

Figure 4.27

The victim should begin on all fours, with a large open target and a flat back to start with. He makes eye contact with the attacker, then, as her foot makes kick contact, he reacts with not only brilliant acting but a contraction of the spine and isolation of the stomach. This kick has a contact knap much like the stomach-punch knap (fig. 4.27).

Kneeling Face Kick

This kick only works with the victim's back to the audience, as this flattens the audience's perspective and masks the contact knap placement. The victim kneels with hands cupped and over-lapping slightly, about a foot in front of her chest. Her palms should be facing out and down (see fig. 4.28) She makes eye contact with the attacker; this gives him the cue to begin moving in for the kick. When the attacker kicks the victim's hands, she reacts by snapping her head straight back like a PEZ dispenser.

The victim should be sure to keep her hands from being too far flung (the same precaution used in the Diagonal Slap)—but use them to "cover the pain." Also, both partners should take a moment to check in and make sure the victim's hands are set correctly before any kicking commences, or she could get kicked in the chest or the face. Ouch!

Figure 4.28

The motion of this kick is exactly like the motion for the kneeling stomach kick, except that instead of kicking the victim's stomach, the attacker kicks her set hands. This technique actually works best when partners begin out of distance. The attacker makes eye contact, takes a step, brings the top of his foot (not the toe) through the victim's cupped hands, and follows through. At no time does the kicking leg fully extend. *Major Safety Tip:* The kick goes straight through the victim's hands, which are placed at least a foot away from her body or face. Do not let the attacking energy (and therefore the kick) move in toward her body at any time. This technique works with both partners far away from each other—it looks to the audience as though they are close enough for contact because perspective gets flattened by the placement of the victim facing directly back. For this technique (really for stage combat in general), it's a good idea when attacking to keep your eyes on targets, not locked on your partner's eyes, after the initial checking-in moment of eye contact. Movements tend to follow the eyes, so focusing on targets that are outside the body will usually ensure that strikes land outside the body.

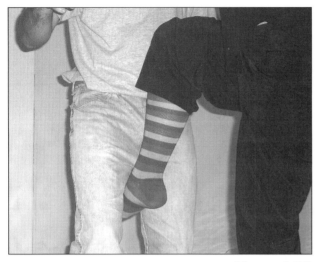

Figure 4.29

Ye Olde Groin Kick: Nothing says physical comedy like a good old-fashioned kick to the groin. There are two ways to do this kick without damaging our precious privates:

1. The same light-but-loud kick with the top of the foot we've been doing, this time to the upper inner thigh (see fig. 4.29). It's a big muscle group, so it doesn't cause pain or damage, but it looks like it's, shall we say, more centrally located.

2. What they call the "British" groin kick is useful for close and/or in-the-round audiences. Using a loose, floppy ankle (as usual), the attacker creates a space between the bend in her ankle and the victim's crotch, so she should be able to kick her partner in the buttocks, behind the groin. This version is a difficult one to master, so be careful, wear a cup, or just use the first version instead!

Boinking

No, it's not what you think. This is the subtle art of acting pain while waiting for the next piece of choreography to commence. For example, I've just been fake-pushed to the floor. While my partner travels toward me to head-slam me, I moan and groan and attempt to crawl away (fig. 4.30). Boinking can also be a great way to get yourself in position for the next bit of choreography, in case you have too many "boxing-ring circles" (two boxers circling each other in endless boring circles between attacks) going on between phrases.

Figure 4.30

Grappling and Pulling Techniques

The following techniques have to do with partnered *isolation*, meaning movements centered around one small isolated body part. Isolation games really exercise the victim being in control—one person feels a hand on his shoulder and instantly isolates a reaction in that shoulder. The game at the end of this section is a good exercise not only for these grappling and pulling techniques, but for general spatial awareness as well, and can be adapted to include all manner of isolation exercises or technique repetition practice.

Hair Pull: The attacker makes the ASL letter *e* with her hand and places it on the victim's head,[8] then she'll *zhuzh* her hand so that the victim's hair is mussed around it but *not* gripped by any fingers. Then all she has to do is follow the victim's movements, acting brilliantly. When the attacker's hand touches the victim's head, the victim will isolate her body's movements around that spot. A common way to ensure that it's the victim doing the moving around, not the attacker pushing, is to have the victim place one or both of her hands over the attacker's for stability. At any time, the victim should be able to walk away without being tangled up in the attacker's fingers (see fig. 4.31).

Figure **4.31**

Don't have any hair? Do the same thing with an ear, a nose—palm the victim's bald head like a basketball. The key is to let *the victim be in control* (yes, I will be repeating this ad nauseam throughout the entire chapter—deal with it), and be sure the attacker's fingers never actually hook into or attach to any part of the victim's anatomy. Ears can rip off pretty easily, remember. Another variation is to do this same hair-pull concept with a shirt front, lapels, or other clothing item.

Pushes: Begin pushing each other around by learning the forward push first, then moving on to backward, then freeform pushes. Be sure that partners always make eye contact before a push technique—it'll help them stay in sync with each other and stay safe. Did I mention the victim is always in control? For a *forward push*, the attacker should step up behind his partner, slightly to the side so that his brilliant acting can be seen, and place his open hands on her shoulder blade without hooking fingers at all, but keeping the hands flat (fig. 4.32). Partners, make eye contact.[9] The attacker does not actually push her, not even softly, but follows her movement as she cocks back and flings her own self forward, isolating the contacted shoulder. If partners choose to add a forward fall to this bit (hey, you're choreographing!), make sure the victim knows her forward fall very well. As she falls, the attacker *must not* assist her by pushing, but will flick his hands off her shoulder as if brushing dust off her shirt. The energy of the flick will look like a powerful push, but in fact will not be directed in to the victim's body at all, but off into the air (fig. 4.33).

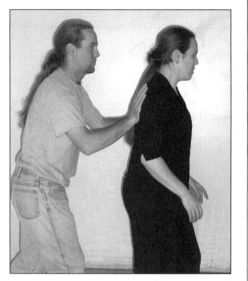

Figure 4.32

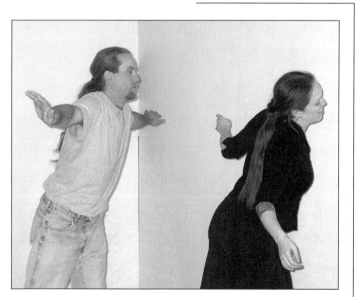

Figure 4.33

For a *backward push*, the attacker will place her hands softly and loosely on the victim's chest, just under the collarbones on the pectoral muscle (see fig. 4.34). Don't forget to make eye contact. The attacker then flicks her hands off upward and to the sides, as though she's flicking lint off her partner's shirt (see fig. 4.35). She *does not* push into her partner's chest, however lightly—the victim is in control. The flicking motion will look like a real push and will let the victim isolate and react in time with the flicking movement, without any actual push momentum affecting his reaction at any time. Both

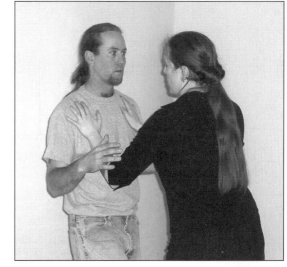

Figure 4.34

partners: Once you get the forward and backward pushes down, practice other angles, other sides, one- or two-handed pushes. Connect the falls you already know to these pushes. Work your way slowly up to speed.

Choke: Never is the isolation and control of the victim more important than in the choke

Figure 4.35

technique. Most importantly, the attacker's hands should never touch the victim's throat. Ever. It'll look real, don't worry; the technique provides an invisible "safety cone" of space between the victim's throat and the attacker's hands, which both partners should guard against slips.

The attacker begins by flicking both hands at the same level and past the victim's ears, really throwing the energy beyond his head. Then the attacker draws her hands back and places them in a cupped "V" on his sternum (*not* around the victim's neck) (see fig. 4.36). As the victim reacts, the attacker follows, never letting that safety cone of her hands slip upward. When the attacker's hands reach the victim's chest, the victim arcs his chin up and over the apex of the V. There should be a large space now between the safety cone and the victim's neck. The victim then grabs the attacker's wrists and isolates—in real life, a person's body curls around pain, or in this case, the suffocation point on the throat (fig. 4.37).

There can be a prearranged cue for detachment, but if both partners are connected properly, with attention and isolation, just the victim letting go should be impetus enough. As far as sound goes, remember: You're being choked. This means your air is getting cut off. So you won't be vocalizing, and will be making minimal coughing and hacking sounds. The less air you've got, the less noise you'll be able to make (see fig. 4.38).

Figure **4.36**

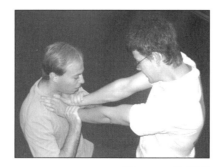

Figure **4.37**

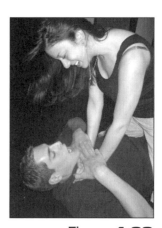

Figure **4.38**

Another variation is the *choke from behind*. The safety-cone concept still applies, except that this time, the attacking arm reaches around the victim's body to be placed on the chest. The victim then turtles her chin all the way forward over the attacker's elbow, masking the cone of safety (see figures 4.39 and 4.40).

Figure 4.39

Figure 4.40

Head Slam: The Head Slam involves a pumping motion before the victim's head actually gets slammed. Make the faster snap-back of the head the last of a three count (bob head so forehead touches placed hand, then raise again: one . . . two . . . fast slam three), or just bob once and slam. Either works. The magic Rule of Three tends to be more comedic. (See the glossary entry "Rule of Three." The basic premise is that three repetitions of anything is funny.) Just be sure both partners agree on which count they're using before the technique begins, or chaos can ensue! The basic Head Slam takes place with the victim on the floor face down, head facing the audience. The Standing Head Slam will be described also—this one is spectacularly violent, especially when the victim has long hair!

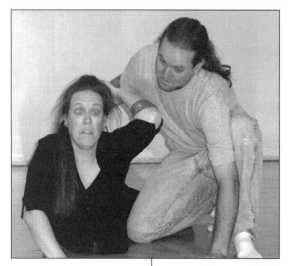

Figure 4.41

As the victim staggers to the floor, she'll place one flat hand palm down on the floor in direct line with her forehead. The attacker will make his way toward her menacingly, kneel, and place one soft hand on her shoulder, one on her head (using the safe placement we learned in the hair pull). This is the victim's cue: The attacker will follow her movement as she bobs her head and flick his hand off her head as she slams. The victim places her forehead on her set hand once or twice, whichever count the partners chose, and presses up all the way with her supporting arm. This is a good opportunity for you hams to mug to the audience. Go for it! For the slam effect, the victim snaps her head fast in the same head-bobbing motion as the windup. The floor hand is there in case the victim's forehead gets too close to actually hitting the floor, but ideally her head will actually snap about an

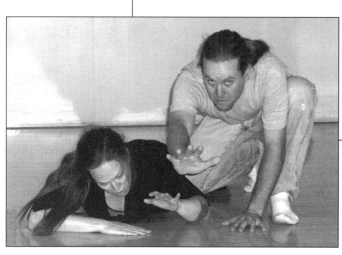

Figure 4.42

Figure 4.43

inch or so above her hand. Important for a good Head Slam is the bobble-head effect afterward: Once the victim has snapped, a head-bobble like one of those annoying toys must be added before she sags to the floor. For a Head Slam knap, the victim slaps the floor with the nonsupporting hand (see figs. 4.41, 4.42, and 4.43).

Safety Tip: The victim is the one doing all the bobbing and slamming. She doesn't need any help, especially when the attacker flicks his hand away from her head—it will look as though her head is slammed into the floor. Remember that any attacking energy should not be directed downward or into her head at any time.

The *Standing Head Slam* is much the same. The setup is like the knee-to-stomach: The attacker places her hand on the victim's shoulder and the other on her head. The victim bobs the set amount, then at the slam the attacker will flick her hand off the victim's head and slap her own thigh. The victim will head snap and bobble as with the floor Head Slam. This could be an easy follow-up to a stomach kick or hair pull.

Grappling: To put safe grappling onstage, the only thing you really need is communication between partners. If both partners can work together, using safe hand placements, isolation, and keeping the victim of each shifting motion in control, grappling can be not only a realistic wrestling-like option, but even a safety

Figure 4.44

Figure 4.45

net. It's common among actor-combatants to agree to meet in a grapple when one or the other has forgotten choreography, or when something very wrong has happened, like a broken sword. Actors can easily speak to each other while grappling without being heard by the audience—they can plan the next move, remind each other of forgotten choreography, or just agree to a good push-and-fall combination to end the fight (see fig. 4.44).

A *tackle* is a variation on the general rules of grappling: The attacker makes eye contact, then runs straight at the victim's very open, set stomach target, not hitting or pushing him even lightly, but slapping his lat muscle or just making a big acting deal of stopping short. The victim places his hands on the attacker's back as a cue, isolating in the middle à la the stomach punch. Then the victim is free to do a safe backward fall or other choreography without hurting the hunched-over attacker (fig. 4.45).

Isolation Game

Have the group of actors take a walk around the room. Encourage fast, slow, lopsided, different-leveled walks. Then the teacher or director calls out "Isolate!" and then a body part. Each actor must either grab or be grabbed by whomever is closest to him, using the called body part. It happens quickly, so this exercise really helps the thinking-on-your-feet aspect of grappling and safe partnering.

Stick Together,[10] an exercise on which this game is based, would actually be a good warm-up either leading to this game or on its own; instead of calling out an isolation, the director or teacher calls out "Stick Together" and a body part, like, say, "bottoms" or "feet." (See figs. 4.46 and 4.47.) Actors must attach to whoever is closest by the called body part. Either of these games is effective starting with walking and then later trying running, skipping, galloping, even leaping through the space.

Figure **4.46**

Unarmed Combo

Let's put some of this unarmed jazz together! Now we have a vocabulary of different moves useful for unarmed stage combat, but a fight isn't a fight until it tells a story to an audience. Here is a standard unarmed sequence to practice. Once you are very comfortable with all the separate techniques and can freely isolate well, try putting together your own sequences and see which combinations make for effective fights.

Figure **4.47**

Unarmed Combo	
ACTOR A:	**ACTOR B:**
Place hands on B shoulder	Cue shoulder back
Flick hands	Isolate shoulder forward, then forward fall
Act!	Boink while placing hand for Head Slam
Place hands for Head Slam cue	Isolate shoulder and head, raise face, mug like crazy!
Follow	Pump head twice
Flick hand	Snap head and bobble
Appear smug	Bobble head, moan to collapse

Conclusion: Style Points

Eastern and Western styles of unarmed stage combat look as different as the cultures they represent, but in truth they use the same basic movements. It's the *style* that makes a punch look like John Wayne or Jackie Chan has thrown it. In order to be versatile and safe, actors should learn the techniques and engage in neutral training. Keep the techniques themselves without character, making them "an empty vessel into which a character may be poured."[11]

After you've got the neutral techniques down smoothly and at stage speed, you can experiment with making changes for style: Block a punch Bruce Lee–style and cowboy-style (one is upright, one more bent and sloppy looking); see how small a change can be the difference between a kung fu flick and a mobster's sucker-punch. Look into martial arts stances and sounds, and compare them with a cowboy's swagger or a sci-fi fake throw (à la Captain Kirk or Dr. Who). Watch some clips and imitate what you see, changing little things for style, but keeping the core technique.

Fundamental Stage Combat Style Differences: Unarmed

1. Character Stance: upright vs. slouched. A boxer dances around, upper body foremost, shielding his face with his boxing gloves (see fig. 4.48). A martial artist poses in a stance from her school/country of study (see fig. 4.49). A cowboy stands with his hands near his holsters, in cowboy boots. A Renaissance-era fencer will salute before combat, a martial artist will bow. Much of stance has to do with era, costume, and character status as well as culture.

2. Unarmed Technique Variations: A "good ol' left hook" punch works much the same as a parrot punch, only the fist actually is curved toward the victim's face a bit, often choreographed to catch and curl around a forearm block.[12] Different martial arts, depending on the country and school of origin, use different hand weapons besides the fist, such as half-fist, edge of hand (bent or straight), palm, clawlike finger positions, all fingers that meet at a point, an open hand, or extended pinky of doom. If you are doing a show that includes martial arts techniques, do your research and see which hand weapons and stances existed in your setting of choice.

Figure 4.48

These are, of course, not the only ways to showcase style. Just remember that the way a character attacks and defends herself is more about *who* the character is than *what* her combat system of choice is. A rich landlady will slap her servant very differently from the way that servant will slap his shrewish wife at home. If you are comfortable with these unarmed techniques in a neutral style, the character herself will come out in the choreography without artificial laying on of style.

That being said, a musketeer of the late 1600s will throw a punch much differently than a Victorian gentleman, so do research your show's setting, both the culture and the period. As previously stated, the costumes themselves will tell much about how a character will move in general, and how he will fight. Having rehearsal costumes for

Figure 4.49

actors is essential, no matter what era the show is set in. This way, corsets and frock coats and shoes and the like (not to mention when we get to weapons and their holsters) aren't an added danger to the staged fight later. At least, nobody will be surprised!

---

1   "Anything I say three times is true."—Lewis Carroll, *Through the Looking Glass*.

2   Having said this, be sure when repeatedly punching anything, even a soft pillow, that your wrist is in proper alignment with your hand—no bent-wrist punches, or the practice will harm more than help!

3   At Metro State College of Denver, a Monty Python–themed scene used third-party knaps with deliberately hilarious results. Terry (the character from *Holy Grail* who wields the coconuts) would provide all knaps with his coconuts, and once when he was late with his scheduled slap sound, he apologized.

4   When punching a victim prone on the floor, one instructor of mine recommended imagining an evil clown face instead of a parrot. This technique, when moved to the floor, called for a larger imaginary target.

5   No parrots or evil clowns were harmed in the making of this book.

6   Some instructors prefer a clap knap for punches in general, but I prefer the more punch-sounding thump of the pectoral-muscle knap. A clap knap sounds too slap-like to me to make a realistic punch sound. Use your best judgment: If it's masked and it's audible, often that's all that's needed.

7   See bird's-egg fist description again, located at the beginning of this section.

8   If you practice this enough, you can hide the fact that you have an open fist—reach out with an open grabbing hand and change to the safety open fist at the last moment.

9   You can do this push safely without the victim twisting around to actually make eye contact, if both partners are connected and following the isolation cues correctly, but I didn't admit that!

10   Read *On the Move* by Ginger Zukowski & Ardie Dickson.

11   Boughn, Jason, "Cross-Sword Puzzles," class lecture, University of Denver, 2001.

12   So *be careful*!

Chapter Five

Sticks and Staffs Will Break My Calves

Probably the most versatile weapon in real-life martial arts is the stick. Why? It comes in all different lengths, looks inoffensive at first glance (umbrellas, brooms, even writing or eating utensils are possible stick-type weapons), and offers a combatant the *option* of how lethal or injurious a technique to use in a given situation. A person who carries a gun for self-defense must either gravely injure or kill an opponent. The same goes for carrying a blade. But with a stick, control over an opponent can be exercised without necessarily leading to such results.[1]

What does this have to do with theatrical combat, in which no one is actually getting hurt? Staffs of all lengths have been used over the centuries by both Eastern and Western cultures, and even the policeman's billy club of today echoes the iron war fans or canes of yesterday. A gentleman of the eighteenth century would never leave the house without his walking stick, a lady of the same time her fan. A farmer of any era and culture would

have around her any number of staffs of many lengths, in the guise of farming tools. Doing a Robin Hood show? Better have a six-foot staff and some solid techniques for both Little John and Friar Tuck, characters we know today as quarterstaff fighters. Sherlock Holmes himself even admits to being a top-notch "single-stick player."[2] Characters of every era and culture use sticks against each other, so that's why the staff is the first weapon we'll wield in this book. Also, holding and using a wooden staff just feels less intimidating and scary than thrusting a steel blade into the hands of an unpracticed beginner.

Conditioning for Staff Work

You are no longer using your own flesh and bone as a weapon—now you're wielding something much harder, and longer, than your arms. Whether you use wood or rattan or bamboo, both the pain and the injury indexes are much higher when wielding a staff than hands alone. Also, the effort involved in wielding a weapon—holding it and moving it with proper control and dynamics—can take a subtle toll on your joints and skin especially, muscles for sure. Here are some exercises and stretches that will help condition you toward wielding stick weapons.

Strikes: Obviously, nobody should be actually striking anyone with a stick in stage combat, but, as in our punch conditioning last chapter, it is important to know what a real strike feels like in order to accurately portray one with a noncontact technique. So, practice the following strike technique, both full contact against a couch or tree and also in the air alone with no target whatsoever. Then, practice "landing" the strikes three to four inches *outside* the same couch or tree.

Figure **5.01**

For a staff *strike* (cane or full-length): Begin in a neutral stance, either *hira ichimonji no kamae* (as shown in fig. 5.01) or any other neutral, natural stance. Look at precisely where you want the staff to strike, then *slide* the staff in your hands until the front arm is extended and the back end of the staff is even with your back elbow. Your front hand will be approximately the same distance from your back hand as your back hand is from the end of the staff.

As you practice the basic strike movement over and over again, make sure you are learning control of the weapon. The staff should not wiggle at the end of the strike; both hands should be relaxed enough to avoid soreness and allow for the sliding motion necessary for proper striking technique, but not so loose that the stick flies out of your hands. Repetitive practice not only makes you more and more comfortable holding and using a weapon as though it's second nature for you, but also (if you pay attention to detail as you go) can teach your body memory the basic movements you'll need for nearly all staff techniques later. Plus, it's fun and you can pretend you're the Kurgan or a cool Shaolin monk practicing on your own time. Soon, grasshopper, you will have an opponent . . .

Figure **5.02**

Stretches: The best thing to do with your stick for stretching is to hold it evenly with both hands and do *side bends*, then bring the stick behind your legs and roll slowly down into a forward hang, giving the stick gentle pulls when you're down there. Both are great for the back and hamstrings (see fig. 5.02). Challenge yourself by doing some of your rolls while holding the staff—it not only gives you spatial awareness of how to hold and place the weapon in unusual circumstances, but also gives you an idea of how much more space you take up when wielding as opposed to when you're unarmed. Be careful as you experiment with different movements, and record your discoveries in your journal. One-handed cartwheel, anyone?

First Aid: Though (as mentioned before) we hope nobody is actually going to get hit for real when using stick weapons in a theatrical setting, accidents can and do happen. Even though a staff weapon is unlikely to break the skin, a good miss can bruise an actor up pretty badly (and we all know or can imagine how much a nasty rap on the knuckles with a piece of wood hurts). Be sure to have ice on hand, and using your leather swordplay gloves can't hurt either. There are some spots that can have serious consequences if hit with a stick: the temples, the nerve point just under the ribs where they meet the sternum and xyphoid process,

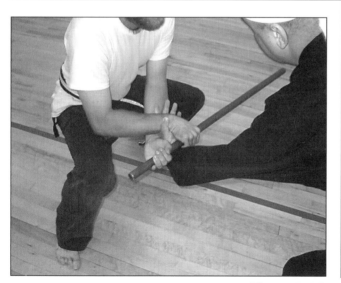

Figure **5.03**

and, of course, anything on or near the eyes or teeth. Just because your staff is made of wood, not steel, doesn't mean it isn't capable of causing serious injury. Also, just because it is a stage combat weapon does not mean it is a toy. A staff is a weapon, whether it's oak or rattan. Be respectful of the danger involved and don't goof around.

Helping Bruises: If you do get yourself whacked with a stick and incur bruising, use a soothing salve to speed healing, and cover with clothing, tape, wristbands, etc., until the bruise is yellow and nearly healed.

Weapon Requirements

The European quarterstaff in the medieval and Renaissance eras ranged from six feet long to nine feet, and was measured based on the user's height. In stage combat, a quarterstaff should be a standard six feet long and an inch in diameter. A cane-style staff (*hanbo* in Japanese martial arts) should be three feet long and three-quarters of an inch in diameter. Materials that are durable enough for stage use include: rattan, bamboo, hard woods like oak, or waxwood (which many martial arts staffs use).

Some stage combat practitioners prefer a lighter rattan or bamboo staff for stage work, especially the six-foot variety. Rattan can look like solid wood but is much lighter in weight. If smacked with a rattan staff, the pain/bruise factor is much less than with a hard wood staff. Either heavier wood or lighter rattan is safe for stage combat, but I'd recommend not combining the two materials. All actors wielding staffs should use all one or the other; I personally have had a rattan staff broken over my head by a wielder of an oak staff, who came down too hard on the much lighter material. I suffered no injury (or contact) at all, however. Just be warned.

Where to Get 'Em: You can choose to purchase staffs from specialty martial arts stores/Web sites (see the resources list for some good places), but I prefer just going to my friendly neighborhood hardware store and perusing the dowel rod section. It's much cheaper that way, and I have practiced full-contact martial arts staff work with my dowel staff with no problems at all. Be sure when going the hardware-store route that you avoid buying pine, as it is a soft wood that breaks easily. Choose oak or a similarly hard wood instead, and be sure to sand it thoroughly when you get it home. Dowels, unlike ready-made martial arts staffs, can give you wicked splinters otherwise. Hey, you're in the hardware store already—buy fine-grain sandpaper (and some stain for a nice dark look if you'd like) and make a staff-preparing day of it.

Wielding

Now you are wielding a weapon: Your arms are extended beyond their normal range, and made of a harder substance, too! Though unarmed techniques can be quite dangerous (check the slap-related injury list one more time—it can't hurt, er, does hurt, well, you know what I mean), but it's obvious that wielding a weapon can and does hurt both more easily and just more than a fleshly weapon alone. A big reason for this is not so much the harder or more dangerous materials themselves, but the fact that most people in this day and age are not accustomed to carrying or using a weapon at all, let alone a full-sized one like a sword or even a cane-sized staff. But as recently as the nineteenth century, men (and some women) were not considered fully dressed without their weapon on, whether they knew how to use it expertly or not at all. Therefore, not only the amount of personal space, but also the actual physical size of folks, was much bigger than now. Carry a golf umbrella with you every day for a week and you'll see what I mean.

Who is your character? An eighteenth-century nobleman who wears a smallsword just for show? A samurai? Are you allowed by your extant society to openly carry a weapon, or must you carry a disguised or hidden one? Questions like these are important to ask as you begin to make yourself comfortable wielding. Your own comfort level with a weapon must be appropriate and realistic for the character you play. Viola from *Twelfth Night* will not be comfortable even touching a weapon, whereas for Mercutio or Tybalt from *Romeo and Juliet*, a weapon is second nature.

Figure **5.04**

What is your reaction when a weapon is drawn, even if not on you directly? In too many Shakespearean productions, I've seen one character draw his sword and all others onstage just stand there unfazed, waiting for the choreography to commence. This is ridiculous! How would you react if your best buddy suddenly pulled out a loaded gun in a crowded room? Freeze in terror, maybe panic. You would not act as though this happens all the time (unless it does). So just because the *actors* have rehearsed this scene a million times and all know what will happen next, the *characters* do not. Neither does the audience. Keep the *danger* immediately in mind when acting and wielding, or around a wielder. And keep your awareness sharp, so you don't involuntarily become an unfortunately wounded bystander.

All staff techniques shown are geared toward a standard six-foot staff, which is commonly used in both Western- and Eastern-style combat. Most of the following techniques can be easily modified to the three-foot staff as well. But as usual, when first learning the basics, practice in a neutral style until you're comfortable with the movements and neutral dynamics involved. I have chosen terms that are sometimes in French, Italian, or Japanese, but don't let that throw you into thinking they must be done in a particular culture's style—they are merely the old martial arts terms that most thoroughly and commonly relate to the stance or movement named. I could have renamed them all in common English, but why do so when they are so aptly named already?

Etiquette

Observing proper etiquette when handling or even just holding a weapon is essential not only for safety, but for learning an innate respect for the dangerous activity in which you are about to engage. Awareness is the first rule of wielding: Know where your weapon is at all times—not only its position in relation to you and your partner, but to everyone around you (and the walls of the room or trees of the park you're practicing in). "Oops, sorry, I didn't see you there" doesn't exist in the world of wielding.

Always bow to your weapon before the first time and after the last time you use it. It's not a religious (or necessarily an Asian or martial arts) thing; what a simple bow to the weapon does is focus your attention on the dangerous object in your hands and offer respect for the dangerous object and practice to come. If you just take a second to bow, you are much less likely to treat the weapon cavalierly, or to have a scattered spirit while you wield it.

If you are holding your weapon but not using it at the moment, hold it with one end touching the ground or your foot, keeping it approximately perpendicular to the floor. Never wave the weapon around between techniques—it's still a weapon, even though you've stopped acting. Never cross the plane of anyone's face with the point of the weapon (this is obviously especially important for sword work, but don't forget this rule when working with your staff as well).

To put your weapon down or away, do not drop or throw it. The only exception to this rule is if you are practicing a disarm technique, in which case we all assume that you are hyper-aware of your weapon's position at all times. Place at least one knee on the floor and put the weapon down softly and quietly. Again, it's a

Figure **5.05**

Figure **5.06**

mark of respect for the weapon, and you'd be surprised how much longer any weapon stays in good shape when treated this way (fig. 5.05).

Stances

En Garde: Stand straight upright, one foot forward, the back foot pointing 45 degrees out. Hold the staff firmly but not too tightly, forward hand facing in, back hand facing out. Your body should be facing three-quarters forward. As described in the "Strikes" section, your forward hand should be almost halfway down the staff, your back hand about a foot away from the end. Point the staff either directly forward or slightly upward, as in fig. 5.06.

Hira Ichimonji No Kamae: This is a simple, unassuming stance (don't let the long Japanese name fool you). Stand straight, facing squarely front, holding the staff firmly but not too tightly in both hands. Your palms should both be facing inward toward the body, and your hands should be evenly spaced on either side of the staff's center. Your arms should be relaxed, and hang straight down. Your feet face forward, parallel and evenly spaced (hip-width apart or slightly further is good). (See fig. 5.01.)

Little John: You've seen illustrations of Robin Hood's cohort in countless children's books, no doubt. Remember how he looks? That's right: just like in fig. 5.07. He's standing straight upright, facing forward, maybe one hand on his hip. He's holding his staff with his dominant hand, letting one end of the staff rest gently on the ground. He is ready to enter into *hira ichimonji* as quick as a wink from this even more unassuming posture. He's often got a big goofy smile on his face—Go ahead!—that makes the stance complete.

Spinning and Gripping

Practice these spins and grip-switches on your own for fun and skill-building before putting them into fights with partners. Mix these with your different stances for fancy-looking solo staff moves to impress or nonplus other characters!

Figure **5.07**

One-Handed: It's a simple figure eight that doesn't change grip at all but makes a good spin effect (remember, O baton twirlers, this is stage combat, not a parade and not real kung fu): Merely dip the forward point of the staff down and up (see fig. 5.08), then turn your wrist and dip down and up again (like in fig. 5.09), then turn, rinse, and repeat until everyone around

Figure **5.08**

Figure **5.09**

you is suitably impressed. Think of it as drawing a big infinity sign over and over again in the air in front of you.

Some directors will be tempted, if they have a baton cheerleader or a martial arts competitor or diablo juggler in the cast, to employ fancy toss-and-catch moves within a staff fight. For a stage production, however, I'd highly caution said directors against such things, as the moment an actor lets go of her weapon, she is no longer in direct control over its movement, which is not considered safe stage combat. When a weapon leaves the hand onstage, whether it's a disarm or a toss-and-catch move, the danger index increases a hundredfold. Besides, weapon-juggling is in the same category as the advanced acrobatics in chapter 3: It won't be necessary for most choreography. Simple movements are cleaner looking, are easier for actors to master and perform onstage, and read best to an audience. Plus, simpler is also safer.

Two-Handed: Begin in en garde, a little more sideways-facing than usual. Begin with the staff on your right side, your left (forward) hand holding palm upward, your right (rear) hand holding palm downward (see fig. 5.10). Ready?

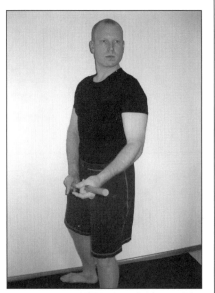

Figure 5.10

1. Let go of your right hand, dip the back end of the staff down to the floor, arcing it toward the body, then the floor, and forward. Catch the staff with the right hand behind the left hand, this time palm downward (fig. 5.11).

2. Continue the circle being drawn by letting go of your left hand and placing it behind your right as the staff's rotation is complete (fig. 5.12). Use your newly placed left hand to guide the staff through a sweeping strike that will switch stance sides for you (as in fig. 5.13). You should end up in the sideways en garde with the staff on your left side this time (as in fig. 5.14).

3. Rinse, speed up, and repeat, going the exact opposite way on the other side till it looks like a smooth, continuous move and you are oh-so-cool looking.

Figure 5.11

Figure **5.12**

Figure **5.13**

Figure **5.14**

This is pretty complex to try to wrap your brain around, but once your body gets the almost figure-eight-like rhythm, it's like riding a bicycle. Except that you don't need to wear a helmet. Well, actually, you might . . .

Staff Grip-Switch: Begin in *hira ichimonji*. Let go with your right hand, and flip it so that it is palm up, underneath the staff, right next to your left hand (see fig. 5.15). Continue to lift the staff with your right hand and guide the staff as it rolls all the way over the back of your left hand (see fig. 5.16) and around (see fig. 5.17). Catch the staff as it comes around, as in fig. 5.18. Now you're in position to do it again but with opposite hands.

Safety Tip: You are holding the staff in two hands at all times during this spin. This keeps the staff within your control and also makes it easier to quickly and smoothly get to a strong stance, which is useful when including spins in fight choreography.

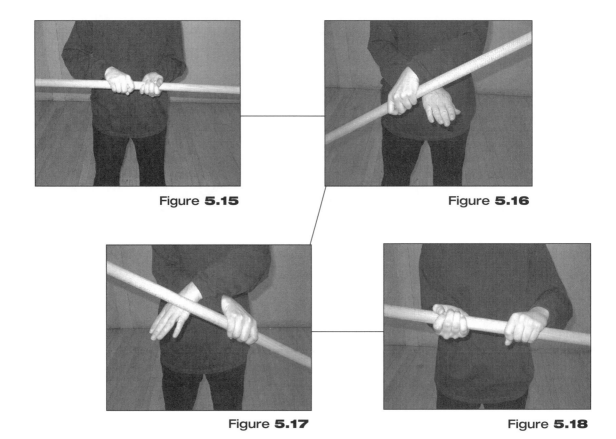

Figure **5.15**

Figure **5.16**

Figure **5.17**

Figure **5.18**

Strikes and Blocks

There are two basic ways to strike with a staff. For the first way, reread the strike technique described under "Conditioning" earlier in this section. We'll call this a plain *strike*. You can strike for targets at the ankle, hip, shoulder, head, and groin, and have the same motion for each, with this exception: An overhead (head) strike or underhand (groin) strike actually works less like a cut from the side and more like a glancing axe chop.

The second way to strike with a staff is slightly different in dynamic and is called a *thrust*. Where a strike has more of a cutting motion, a thrust is a direct hit with the end of the staff, a piston-like motion. Both kinds of strikes involve sliding the staff in the hands to extend for the hit illusion, but the strike is a cutting swish with the side and the thrust is a poke with the end, like shooting pool.

Practice alternating strikes and thrusts with your tree/couch/kicking bag. As in the conditioning sections, practice full contact to get the feel of it, then practice stage combat targets, which are three to four inches *outside* the body.

Safety Tip: Strikes should never have energy directed in toward the victim's body, just like in unarmed techniques. Neither should a thrust; hence, the targets are about four inches outside the body and never in contact!

There are also two ways of blocking with a staff. The first actually works the same way the plain strike does: an extension of the staff through a slight slide of the staff through the hands, to block a strike instead of deliver one. Instead of aiming for a target to hit, extend and meet an opponent's incoming strike. When practicing this alone, you won't see much of a physical difference between the plain strike and the plain block, so make sure the intention when doing them is very clear.

The second type of block is what I call a *reinforced block*. I call it this because it looks a lot like the reinforced parry some instructors use in rapier techniques. The reinforced block is used perpendicular to the floor for shoulder strikes, parallel for head and groin strikes. Instead of taking the strike with an end of the staff, with a reinforced block, the incoming strike will land in the center of the staff, between the hands. The important thing to remember about the reinforced block is to keep the ends of the staff away from your partner at all times. When practicing solo, be hyper-aware of the ends of the staff. To control the ends of the staff, practice the window-shutter motion with the shoulder-strike block: From the stance of your choice, shift and bring the staff perpendicular to the floor, off to one side. Imagine closing a sliding-glass door or a window and move the still-perpendicular staff across your body to meet the incoming shoulder strike.

Safety Tip: Place your reinforced block a bit forward for both the head and groin-strike blocks, or you could end up getting whacked. Hopefully your attacker won't have his intention coming in toward your body, but it pays to be safe on both ends.

The Drill

What follows is a fundamental drill for staff work. Learn both attacker and defender sides as you learn and practice solo; then when you meet with a partner and put them together, they'll be smooth and you'll be able to switch roles seamlessly as you drill. Altogether it can look and definitely feel like a fight when you have it smooth and to speed. Of course, the parts to this drill are in fact the building blocks for fundamental staff fight choreography.

Solo: Attacking (from en garde)

1. Strike ankle L (fig. 5.19)
2. Strike ankle R (fig. 5.20)
3. Strike hip L (fig. 5.21)
4. Strike hip R (fig. 5.22)
5. Thrust shoulder L (fig. 5.23)
6. Thrust shoulder R (fig. 5.24)
7. Overhead strike head (fig. 5.25)
8. Underhand strike groin (fig. 5.26)
9. Swipe*

Solo: Defending (from en garde)

1. Low block L (fig. 5.19)
2. Low block R (fig. 5.20)
3. Med-low block L (fig. 5.21)
4. Med-low block R (fig. 5.22)
5. Reinforced block at L shoulder (fig. 5.23)
6. Reinforced block at R shoulder (fig. 5.24)
7. Reinforced block overhead (fig. 5.25)
8. Reinforced block forward from knees (fig. 5.26)
9. Evade*

*This is the exception to the no-crossing-the-plane-of-the-victim's-body rule, because the actors are actually farther away even than standard safe distance when doing a swipe/avoid combo. The illusion is that the attacker is attempting to smack the defender with a wide, hard strike, and the defender evades according to the height level of the incoming strike.

There are three basic levels to this attack-and-evade combo:

Low-Level Swipe	
(cut the feet off)	
ACTOR A:	**ACTOR B:**
Eye contact	Ditto!
Place end of staff on ground	Jump, in a tuck or cross-legged position
Drag staff along ground, between you & partner	Watch your staff-ends as you jump and land

Mid-Level Swipe	
(hip or stomach level)	
ACTOR A:	**ACTOR B:**
Eye contact	Ditto!
Wind up	Place staff and hands safely to prepare (overhead is good)
Bring staff tightly to body, swipe close to own body	Make "hup" sound and avoid, scooting feet backward, contracting stomach

High-Level Swipe	
(decapitation level)	
ACTOR A:	**ACTOR B:**
Eye contact	Ditto!
Wind up	Deep plié to crouch (don't duck, keep spine straight)
Swipe straight across where partner's head *used* to be, tight in to your own body	Watch your head!

When doing the drill, choose ahead of time which level or sequence of levels you'll do for the final move, then come back in distance and do it again!

Safety Tip: Attackers, be sure you always send your energy past your victim's body, not into it. This is especially important to remember in the overhead strike! It's not a full-on axe chop, but should glance off the block. It feels a lot like a fly-fishing cast, actually.

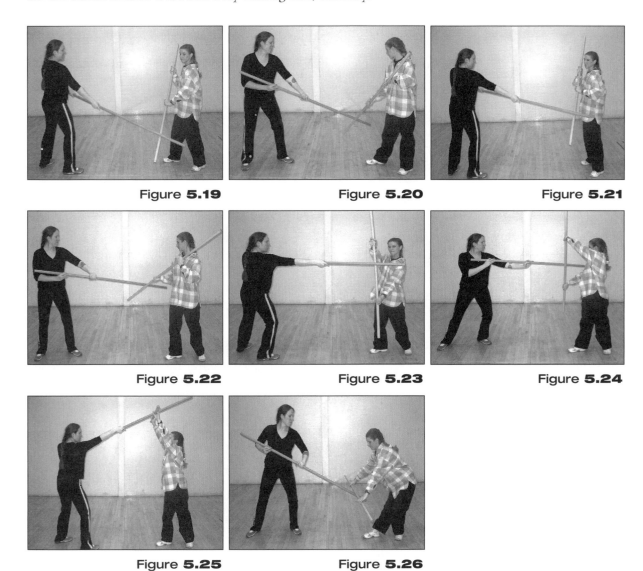

Figure **5.19**   Figure **5.20**   Figure **5.21**

Figure **5.22**   Figure **5.23**   Figure **5.24**

Figure **5.25**   Figure **5.26**

Staff Meeting: Partnered Drill

It's a simple matter of putting it together: By now I'm sure you can see how the two halves that comprise the solo drills fit together. Go slowly until you get used to the give-and-take and are in tune with your partner. Use eye contact, and remember, it is okay to talk to each other!

Once you have the halves meeting together in a smooth partnered drill with a smooth transition of switching roles after each final swipe, gradually and carefully speed it up until you are at a good stage speed.[3]

Footwork: Once you are smooth operators with the drill in partners, have the attacker move forward and the defender move backward as the drill progresses. Can you keep safe distance while moving together? See how many times you can go back and forth across the space without making a mistake!

Figure 5.27

Style Points

One final staff-fighting note: You (or your director) will no doubt have done research on the setting and cultural context of the show in which your staff fight is to appear. The basic moves aren't all that different between East and West, at least not in their basic forms. Etiquette, attitude, costume, and stance flair will be the difference the audience sees. And, as always with wielding any weapon (including just the hands), the style will have more to do with the *character* who wields the weapon than with an artificially imposed look.

1   Read Hatsumi and Chambers' *Stick Fighting*.

2   Watson learns this in "A Study in Scarlet," the first Holmes story by Arthur
     Conan Doyle.

3   There are four basic speeds (in order of slowest to fastest): rehearsal speed
     (which can actually be quarter-, half-, or three-quarters speed), full stage
     speed (natural looking for stage), full film speed (natural looking for camera),
     and Jackie Chan speed. We won't be using the third or fourth speeds
     in this manual.

Chapter Six

European Swords

The rapier is a long, versatile sword used by Europeans from the mid-1500s through the late 1600s. When most folks think of musketeers, Mercutio and Tybalt, swashbuckling, and *The Princess Bride*, they're thinking of the rapier.

Since the rapier is so versatile (used for both edge and point play), easy to wield for nearly all body types, and prevalent in lots and lots of theatre (Shakespeare is only one of many), we will cover rapier techniques in detail exclusively in this chapter to represent European-style swordplay.[1] An overview of two other somewhat common European swords will close the chapter.

Weapon Requirements

It is extremely important that safety be the main concern when choosing a sword for stage use. Don't make the mistake of merely going to an Olympic fencing supplier and buying sport-fencing weapons for stage combat use. Fencing foils are made for touching only, with the point only, and will break under the repetitive strain of rehearsal/class use. Plus, they have much

thinner blades than a real rapier, and so turn invisible onstage, causing confusion in the audience, blind-fighting in the actors. Not good.

Also avoid getting replica swords advertised as "battle ready" and looking like chrome. Most replica swords are made of soft metal that, after a few rehearsals or classes, collect nicks and burrs until they are nearly serrated. Not only costumes are in danger from swords like this—so is your own precious skin. Go ahead and buy one for wall decoration, but if you are ever going to have any contact (including the light contact essential for stage combat), you need to make sure your rapier has the following characteristics:

1. The blade should be flexible as well as strong. When the blade bends, it should snap back to true every time. If it stays bent, it'll break eventually at that bent point. If it doesn't bend at all, it's too brittle for stage use and will shatter on impact.

2. The sword's parts should fit together seamlessly, with no gaps between parts and no fillers to fill up said gaps. A loose, jangly sword is a dangerous one. Most important, the tang (see "Parts o' the Rapier," below) should go all the way through the handle to the pommel, should screw into the pommel in such a way that there'll be no thread-stripping, and should be all steel (including the pommel).

3. The sword should be dismantleable. If you can't take it apart and fit it back together just as well, it's probably not put together properly. You should be able to take the whole thing apart, clean it, and put it all back together with no loose bits and no shims or other fillers to make it tight.

4. The sword should have what's called a "schlager" blade.[2] This is my own professional opinion, and I'll tell you why: First, the blade itself has

a diamond- or lozenge-shaped cross-section, which not only looks period-extant, but catches the light onstage, making it easy for the audience and the actors to see. The cross-section described, though it gives thickness for look and good sound, also makes the sword light enough for nearly everyone to wield easily. Third, schlager blades are sturdy and flexible, with a no-nonsense tang. Finally, both the sword cutler and the sword fighter I respect the most swear by schlager blades, so if you don't believe me, believe them![3]

Let's face it: You need to have a real sword for stage work. Not a piece of sports equipment, not a fake or a toy. The flexibility, manufacture, and durability should be as reliable as if you were a seventeenth-century gentleman looking for his daily defense. The only differences between what you need for your work and what Tybalt used in the 1600s are that 1) your rapier will not be sharpened and 2) it will have either a blunt or a buttoned point. That's it. Really. And remember that a fake, badly made sword is much more dangerous than a well-made real one.

Parts o' the Rapier

There are many, with various fun European names. Let's stick with the fundamentals. Here are the parts essential for basic knowledge.

Blade: It's the, um, blade. Yeah. Get a schlager. The various sections of the blade are as follows: the *forte*, the strongest part, which is comprised of the third of the blade closest to the handle; the *foible*, the weakest yet most flexible part, which is comprised of the third of the blade closest to the tip; and the *middle*, which is the, er, middle. Blade play should always meet forte to foible (attacker's foible to defender's forte). Makes sense, right?

Hilt: The steel structure surrounding the hand as the rapier is held. There are many different hilt designs, such as the *cup*, *basket*, *swept*, *double-ring*, and *transitional* hilts. The hilt is meant to protect the sword hand and was also used to block, trap, or even break an opponent's blade. Though we never want to break our partner's blade in stage combat, the rest of it is useful for stage.

There is often a loop underneath the hilt that you hook your index finger through for added control. Not all rapiers have this feature, but a well-made one should. It allows the wielder to hold the rapier properly and gives extra control.

Grip: The handle—the part you hold. It should be wrapped with leather or wire, and should be made of either steel or high-octane nylon. Wooden grips are not terrible (and are quite attractive), but tend to get slippery and damaged.

Tang: The part of the blade (yes, it should be all one piece) that you don't see: It runs into the hilt, through the grip, and attaches to the pommel, hopefully with threads like a screw.

Pommel: That big ornate ball at the butt-end of the sword. It should screw onto the tang tightly and uniformly, and be made of solid steel. The pommel adds to the balance of the rapier and can also be used for *pummeling* an opponent. Get it?

Dimensions and Where to Get 'Em

Correct rapier blade length can be anywhere between thirty-one and thirty-four inches, with a handle between five and eight inches long. So your total rapier length will be somewhere between thirty-six and forty-two inches. The blade thickness will vary depending on your maker and the era you're going for— early rapiers were thick and heavy, later ones were lighter, until they transitioned into the extremely light thrusting weapon, the smallsword. For stage, stick with a relatively light, standard stage schlager blade. It'll be easy to wield for nearly every size of actor and be visible onstage.

As far as where to get them, my favorite sword cutler lives in my neck of the woods, and is named Dennis Graves. His info, along with several others' info, is provided in the Resources section at the back of this book. However, it is very important to remember that you need to be careful when getting stage-ready swords! Check them out; make double and triple sure the swords you're getting are safe and well made enough for the tough work of rehearsal or class. I haven't personally used all of those on my list, so use at your own risk, and be smart!

Conditioning

To get your hands and forearms strong enough for extensive drilling with the rapier, I recommend the "eagle claw" squeeze device martial artists use, or one of those soft stress balls, or any other hand-squeezing device you prefer. Squeeze while you watch TV, read, or chat on the phone and you'll be amazed how much more stamina you'll have later when wielding.

Also, do the wrist exercises from chapter 3. Rapier play is all in the wrist, so it's important to limber up those wrists to stave off soreness later. Other good exercises from taihenjutsu are: yoga (especially the Warrior pose), all stretches (of course), and the arm helicopter.

Stance

If you check out older stage sword-fighting manuals, or Dale Girard's book *Actors on Guard*, you'll see many different stances with as many Italian names. In truth, any way you can think of to hold the darn thing has a name and a precise "way." For this manual, we'll (as usual) stick to the fundamentals. In fact, you only need one very versatile stance as a beginner:

En Garde: Stand with feet shoulder-width apart, one foot slightly in front of the other. Your back foot should be turned out slightly (about 45 degrees). Be sure your hips, shoulders, and face are all facing squarely forward. Though standing sideways may be good for real sword fighting since it shrinks open targets, leaving fewer attack options open to an opponent, it is precisely for this reason that actors do not want to be sideways in a staged fight! You want to face your opponent squarely,

Hey, left-handed folks!

Since the author is right-handed, and the following techniques are based on ancient fighting systems wherein left-handedness was not taken into consideration at all, the rapier techniques will be shown and described right-handed only. But don't fret! Left-handed stage rapier fighters use the same philosophies, stances, footwork, and techniques as their right-handed counterparts, just in a mirror image to them. So if you're left-handed and using this manual, do just what you see here, only the opposite!

clearly showing all your targets so that there are no surprises or fudged moves. Your spine should also remain upright (except for very specific acting or choreography purposes).

Now that your feet and torso are in place, let's see what to do with our arms. Sticking with the basics, we'll place our hands at middle height (you can do this stance either high or low as well), slightly but not fully extended, and relaxed. Since we are starting our basics without a weapon, point your two fingers forward, about four to five inches outside your opponent's shoulder. Remember that in the en garde stance, your forward leg is the same as your sword hand. Your "off" hand, or unarmed hand, should not hang dead at your side, but rather be engaged and active. As we go through different bits of footwork, your off hand will move accordingly. For now, in our still stance, have your off hand either resting on your hip, or actively protecting your face (relaxed at chest level) (fig. 6.01).

Figure **6.01**

Footwork, or the Subtle Yet Deadly Art of the Index Card

While we learn rapier footwork, let's not worry about the rapier at all yet. Get yourself a three-by-five index card, and hold it lightly yet firmly in your sword hand, letting the card rest on your curled index finger with your thumb guiding it on top. This is all the weapon you need . . . for the moment (fig. 6.02).[4]

Figure **6.02**

With any rapier footwork, be sure the horizon doesn't bounce while stepping either forward or backward: Keep your knees slightly bent and imagine carrying a glass of water on top of your index card—don't let any spill! Those familiar with dance terms will find this similar to the low, centered "jazz run."

There are five basic building blocks to rapier footwork:

1. *Advance*: Start in en garde, then step forward with your front foot (not too big a step), then let your back foot follow until you're in en garde again. Some instructors call this a "shuffle step," but students shouldn't think about dragging the back foot like that—it's a bad habit. It should be a light step.

2. *Retreat*: Same as the advance, only backward. Lead with the back foot and let the front foot meet it in en garde.

3. *Pass Forward*: It's a step forward where you end up in en garde with your left foot in front. Starting in en garde, lead with your left (back) foot, and step forward so that your left foot passes your right.

4. *Pass Back*: Just like the pass forward, except, well, backward.

5. *Lunge*: There are actually two sizes of lunge: the demi, or half lunge, and the grand, or full lunge. A lunge is a giant advance without the back foot moving forward to join in en garde (fig. 6.03).

As for your upper body, practice extending the sword arm before you move (usually attacks move forward, so do this when advancing/passing forward for now). This is called *telegraphing*, and it's foolish to do in real martial arts, but essential to stage combat. Why? First of all, you are not trying to surprise your partner. Quite the opposite, in fact—you both need to be on the same page at all times. If you extend your weapon before you move, not only does it cue him to move accordingly with you, but it also gives him an idea how far away you are, how long your arm is, and if you are in fact still in safe distance or if something has happened. All stage combat is like a physical conversation: One partner extends her arm, the other answers by readying a parry. Audiences see this and think, "Oh, I get it!" and if it's happening in stage speed, nobody's the wiser as far as the telegraphing (except the actors, which is a good thing!).

Figure 6.03

One last note about arms: As you practice your lunges, have your off hand shoot either straight behind you or over your head. The former will look natural and also help you keep your balance, and the latter does the same, but is considered a more decorative stance.

More Footwork Stuff

Flick the Quarter: This is a game for lunge conditioning that some sport fencers use. Start in en garde. Place a quarter underneath the big toe of your forward foot. As you step to make the lunge, use your big toe to push the quarter away from you so it glides as far across the floor as possible. Even just visualizing this is good for dynamic, deep lunges, especially for those who feel self-conscious or are not very flexible.

The Tire: Stand in en garde. Using either masking tape or your imagination, draw a giant tire on the floor. Your forward foot

Figure **6.04**

should rest on the inner edge of the tire, your back foot along the outer edge, using your safe distance to determine the tire's size. Arm yourself with your deadly index card, and practice all your footwork, keeping your feet on the tire's edges at all times. Check often to make sure you are beginning and ending each movement with en garde. Work with partners in a couple of ways: First, place a stationary, unarmed partner directly in the center of the tire and circle both directions, keeping your sword arm extended toward her and in safe distance. Second, have both partners stand across from each other on the same tire and circle each other, keeping proper foot alignment in en garde and on the tire (fig. 6.04). This simple circling is useful for pause moments between phrases of choreography: Try some taunting lines while doing it!

Wielding

Now let's add a steel weapon to our stance and footwork. Since the rapier's balance rests mostly on your curled index finger

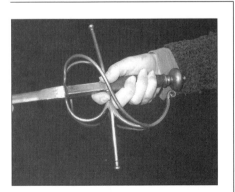

Figure **6.05**

(looped or not), you can feel how much wrist control you have over the weapon (fig. 6.05). You can choose to hold your weapon pronated or supinated, but for now, avoid the "goofinated" hand position, as two rapiers must always meet edge to edge, and it's naturally easy to meet with the flat instead when goofinated. As with the staff work but even more so, be aware at all times where your sword's point is—though a stage weapon, a steel rapier is a steel rapier. Even unsharpened, dull-pointed rapiers are still weapons, and can indeed cause injury.

Etiquette

Reread the "Etiquette" section in the staff chapter again. One more time, why not?

As an etiquette and awareness exercise, always bow to your rapier before the first time and after the last time you use it (just like your staff). Also, before the first time and after the last time you work with your partner, you should salute each other. This practice hails from real-life dueling days, as a courtesy to the person you were about to hopefully skewer. For stage combat practice, it's still a sign of respect, and a tuning-in moment you can have with your partner, to thank him for working with you and to connect before you connect with steel. A basic salute should bring the hilt to your forehead, then the sky, then point your blade down to the ground (fig. 6.06). Feel free to add as many blade-circles as your manner requires. Just remember: *The point of your weapon must never cross the plane of your partner's face.*

Figure **6.06**

As for dress code, avoid overlong sleeves, pockets, plackets, or belt loops, or anything else that can easily catch on your weapon as you learn how to move with it. You should always wear closed-toed shoes and keep hair out of your face for added protection. And finally, invest in soft leather gloves; full-fingered is best. It adds protection to the hands in case of slip-ups, and also keeps the grip from getting slippery. You don't want your sword flying out of your hand as you sweat, and the leather guards against that. And if you are going to be rapier fighting for a show, get the costume (the real one—the one you'll be wearing in performances) as soon as possible. Costumes, especially period costumes, can cause dangerous surprises if you're not fully accustomed to doing these movements with them.

Cut Versus Thrust

There are two basic ways of attacking with a rapier: the *cut* and the *thrust*. A cut is a slicing motion; the intention is to cut the opponent with the edge of the blade. Cue up so that the pommel indicates where the attack will come, then extend and flick the energy past your opponent's body.[5] A thrust is not a slice, but a poking motion, the intent being to stab the opponent with the tip of the blade. Cue up so that the incoming blade is very chambered back and far away from the opponent's body, but the direction of the hilt indicates where the attack will come. Extend and send the energy past your opponent's body.

Practice cutting and thrusting solo, both stationary from en garde, and with the footwork you've learned. Get used to extending the arm before any footwork (or indeed any leaning) occurs—it's an essential habit to start building before you have a real partner in front of you. And don't forget your unarmed hand! Keep it engaged as you move—it doesn't have to be moving too; just be sure it doesn't hang dead at your side as you concentrate on everything else!

Targets

Though the rapier drill directions say things like hip, shoulder, overhead, etc., remember that at no time should your energy go into your partner's body. The actual targets are approximately four inches outside the body, with energy (just like in unarmed, just like in staff) flung past your partner. So a direction such as "cut to right shoulder" really means: Extend the arm and flick a cut about four inches outside your partner's shoulder, with the blade sending energy past her body. And watch where you're aiming! It's a good thing to make eye contact with your partner before beginning a phrase, to make sure everything's hunky-dory and to connect with her before you sling steel at her, but after that, look at your targets! Your body (wise thing that it is) tends to follow your focus, so if you're still looking into your partner's eyes when you cut toward her, guess where that blade will end up. Yikes!

As far as touching blades goes, rapiers should always meet edge to edge, forte to foible. The attacker's foible should, if he is in safe distance, naturally meet the defender's forte (which is realistically sound as well). If you meet rapier blades flat to flat instead of edge to edge, the blades will incur damage and maybe even break, since they're not meant to take force that way. The only exception to the edge-to-edge rule is for spanking and placing the blade for the skin-cut or kill-shot illusion. These techniques require contact with the flat only because they use blade-to-flesh contact, not blade-to-blade.

Finding Distance

Remember "hang loose?" It's the same: Have the partner with the longest arms raise his sword's point outside his partner's body, then slowly and carefully bring the point to touch the extended pinky of his partner (fig. 6.07). This way, the swords are close enough to meet forte to foible, but not close enough to touch anyone! It also looks real to an audience—get any farther away

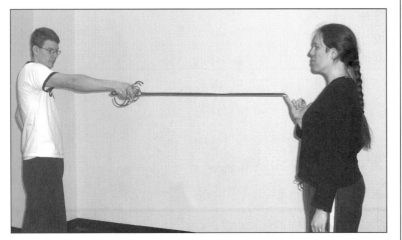

Figure 6.07

than this, and not only will you be missing parries right and left, but the audience will see that you're too far away for realism.

Safety Tip: Be sure you measure distance with a fully extended arm, or you'll end up too close for comfort. Also, if the attacking partner so much as leans forward, let alone advances or lunges forward, the defending partner must match that footwork backward exactly, or safe distance will be closed. No matter who moves where, or how different in body type partners are, the footwork must match.[6]

The Drill[7]

It's best to learn the rapier drill in two separate halves; this way it's easier for the beginning wielder's brain to wrap around it all. There are ten moves in all, so let's begin with one through five:

Solo: Attacking (from en garde)

1. Cut L hip

2. Cut R hip

3. Cut R shoulder

4. Cut L shoulder

5. Overhead cut[8]

Don't do any footwork yet, just be en garde facing each other and lean in and out as you attack and defend. And attackers: Be sure you watch your point as you transition between attacks three and four. Your sword's point should be either pointed straight upward, or you can do a *moulinet*, or "windmill," which drops your point and brings the blade around behind the body to end in a cut to the other side (fig. 6.08).

Figure 6.08

The parries are a bit more complicated to describe. Remember that when parrying, you should place your blade perpendicular to the floor, and let the attack lightly contact your forte. You shouldn't have to reach to meet your partner's blade, nor should you place your parry too far outside your body—four inches is plenty for safety and realism. Finally, when moving from parry to parry in this drill, keep the point of your rapier outside your partner's body at all times, even in transitions. Imagine you are tracing half-circles around your partner, and keep your blade on a flat plane perpendicular to the floor.

Figure **6.09**

Solo: Defending (parry from en garde)

1. Drop the point of your sword to the floor, bring it across your body to guard your L hip. Imagine you're looking at your wristwatch (fig. 6.09).

2. Keeping the sword perpendicular, bring it back across your body to guard your R hip. Your knuckles should face R (fig. 6.10).

3. Circle your point L to R, end up with the blade perpendicular to the floor, point to the ceiling, to guard your R shoulder. Your palm ends up facing forward (fig. 6.11).

4. Keep the sword in the same position, move it across your body to guard your L shoulder. Imagine closing a sliding door. Your knuckles should end up facing L (fig. 6.12).

5. Bring your hilt up above your head so that your blade is horizontal and slightly forward from your head (fig. 6.13). Imagine a windshield wiper.

Practice the first half of this drill many, many times stationary. Once the upper-body moves are smooth, all targets are safe, and the blades are ringing nicely because they are meeting lightly forte to foible, at 90-degree angles every time, *then* add the foot-

Figure **6.10**

Figure **6.11**

Figure **6.12**

Figure **6.13**

work. For now, have the attacker move forward using only advances, and the defender move backward using only retreats. Stop often to check for safe distance—if you get too far away, you'll miss blades. If you get too close, you'll meet blades middle to middle, which isn't good for your safety or the swords'. Be sure you switch attacker and defender roles.

Once this is smooth and feels set in your body, you can move on to the second half of the drill:

Solo: Attacking (from Cut 5)

High 3: Diagonal high shoulder cut: high L to low R (target is the space between the ear and the shoulder. And I mean *space*!)

High 4: Diagonal high shoulder cut: high R to low L

6. Thrust R shoulder

7. Thrust L hip

8. Thrust R hip

At the end of the full drill sequence, you can add a swipe-and-avoid the same way we did for the staff—in fact, the swipe and the avoid work exactly the same way with the rapier as they did with the staff! Be extra-careful with the sword's point, both when attacking and avoiding. You should know where the point of your sword is at all times. As an alternative, you can also swipe diagonally. The avoid for a diagonal swipe is a long sideways lunge (sometimes even with a step added) leading with the head toward the high end of the cut. In other words, if the attacker swipes on the diagonal high right to low left, the defender's avoid will lead with his head to the right (fig. 6.14). You can also add what's called a *waterfall parry* to the diagonal avoid, holding the blade above the avoiding head on the same diagonal as the swipe, so that the swipe will skate along the protective blade and sail harmlessly by (fig. 6.15).

Figure **6.14**

Figure **6.15**

Defending: (from parry 5)

High 3: Angled parry: point up and slightly L, hilt just above shoulder slightly R (fig. 6.16)

High 4: Bring hilt across body like a windshield wiper to an angled parry: point up and slightly R, hilt just above shoulder slightly L (your arm will be across your chest) (fig. 6.17)

Figure **6.16**

Figure **6.17**

6. Keeping the back of the hand facing forward, bring the sword back across your body to guard R shoulder (fig. 6.18). Again, imagine the sliding glass door. And yes, it feels weird to have your palm facing you and the blade perpendicular to the ceiling, but that's how it is.

Figure **6.18**

Figure **6.19**

Figure **6.20**

7. Draw a half-circle with your point until it is pointing to the floor, palm facing forward, to guard L hip (fig. 6.19). Watch your point: Keep the plane of the circle flat. You can also add more circles with your wrist before you end up in the parry position. Doing this is called an *actor's parry*, because it's ridiculously unrealistic but looks super-cool!

8. Keeping your palm facing forward and your point still to the floor, bring your sword back across your body to guard R hip (fig. 6.20). This one feels weird too—if you can't get your wrist to do this safely, you can just end with parry 2 instead of 8.

Again, practice this half of the drill by itself, slowly and in stationary en garde stances until you really do get the hang of it. Then, add it to the first half to get all ten moves down smoothly, together, ending with a swipe-and-avoid of your choice, and switch attacker roles between each drill sequence, also smoothly. Then, and only then, should you practice this entire ten-move drill with your advances and retreats as footwork.

The rapier drill encompasses most basic moves you'll need to have down to put together a safe and realistic European swordfight. In fact, with clear intentions, good technique, and good acting, the drill itself can look like a "real" choreographed fight, particularly when ended with a swipe-and-avoid combination. Can you move your drills, attacker advancing and defender retreating, switching roles after each swipe-and-avoid, smoothly? See how many times you can move your drills back and forth across the room without messing up. Now get it to stage speed. You'll have to do it over and over again; after all, it is called a "drill" for a reason. Once you can do this drill with enough speed and clarity and safety to look good onstage, your rapier vocabulary will be large enough that any fight choreographer will be able to show you choreography and you'll know just what you're doing.

The drills are getting too easy? I doubt it. Okay, if you really think so, try using passes back and forward mixed in with the advances and retreats in your footwork. How is it different in feel and stage picture when your off foot is forward? How does mixing the footwork mess with your safe distance? Go slowly and check your distance often to avoid injury. Try having the attacker retreat and the defender advance. How would this footwork be useful in characterization?

Still too easy? How about putting the drill on the footwork tire? Try going through the whole drill with partners facing each other across the tire, rotating one step each move. Now try combining the circular footwork with the linear advance and retreat footwork. Now have the attacker lunge into attack eight each time. The rapier drill is so versatile and so comprehensive that I'd suggest spending most of your sword time drilling over and over again.

Alternative Rapier Techniques

So now you're a master of the rapier drill. Here are a few of the basic moves not included in the drill that are useful for a wide range of rapier vocabulary.

Parry Alternatives

When putting together rapier choreography, try some of these dynamically different parries for different effects. Like the moves from the drill, these are based on ancient European fighting styles. There are many more than are listed here—these are the fundamentals.

Battre Main, or Hand Parry: Obviously, you want to have your gloves on when you do this one! Instead of parrying an attack with your sword, slap the offending blade away with a relaxed hand. This is one instance where a goofinated attacking hand position is good: This way the hand parry slaps the flat of the blade, not the edge.

Some stage combat instructors suggest a *reinforced parry*, which is the rapier held with both hands—one on the hilt as usual, one holding the blade at the foible—but many choreographers feel this is an unrealistic and silly-looking way of using the hands with the rapier.

Beat Parry: Instead of softly meeting the attacking blade with a parry, hit it hard instead, smacking it farther away from your body. Be sure you don't disarm your partner! You can also use the rapier's hilt to smack an attacking blade away: Try the hilt-slam variation from parry #5 of the above drill.

Waterfall Parry: This was mentioned earlier when we learned the diagonal avoid. You can hold the rapier with just the sword hand, or you can reinforce the parry by holding on with both hands.

Bind:[9] From a parry of two, bring your defending point up until the attacking blade is sitting on your horizontal "shelf." Guide the attacking sword completely around, turning your body until the offending blade is trapped on the floor underneath yours (fig. 6.21). Your partner should follow you, keeping the blades engaged. Make sure you both pay attention to both swords' points! For this bind, be sure to have a completely straight, extended arm and draw a huge circle around the attacker's whole body—if your arm is a little bent or the circle isn't big enough, your point will cross your partner's eyes or face, which is bad. You can also bind from other parries, but the large circle necessary for the low-

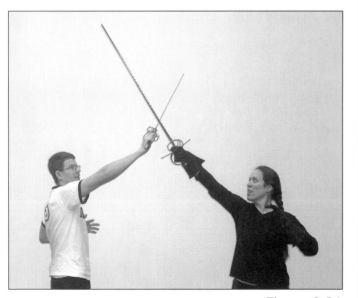

Figure 6.21

parry binds is good practice for beginners, and looks big and dramatic to an audience.

Corps-a-Corps: This literally means "body-to-body." A corps-a-corps is a good resting point for a fight without having to have fighters disengage: Often lines are spoken from a corps-a-corps, and it's also a good way for actors to stop a fight and confer if something onstage goes very wrong. There are many ways to get into a corps-a-corps, but here are two common and simple ones: First, from the bind above, if both partners turn their bodies slightly, they can end up shoulder to shoulder with interlocked swords (fig. 6.22). This is a good place for lines or a shove into the next phrase of the fight. Second, one partner pommel-strikes to high four, and the defending partner catches his wrist. Then the defending partner comes back with the same attack, which the attacking partner catches the same way. Then they can move in close to each other, growl in a menacing manner, taunt each other, or confer to figure out what went wrong in the choreography, and decide what to do next. See fig. 8.1 for an example of this type of corps-a-corps.

Figure **6.22**

Unarmed with a Sword

Rapiers aren't just for cutting, thrusting, and parrying—they're for pummeling and punching too!

Pommel Strike: Doesn't that steel knob at the end of your rapier look nasty? How about if you smacked your opponent in the kisser with it? You can pommel strike just like the parrot punch with a straight jab reaction, or you can stomach punch with the pommel. Obviously, the pommel stomach punch should never be a contact punch.

Knucklebow Punch: Hey, a new vocabulary word! The knucklebow is the part of the hilt that protects the knuckles. In a cup or basket hilt, the entire hilt itself will often extend to become the knucklebow, and in swept hilts and transitional hilts the knucklebow will be a bar that sweeps over the knuckles and meets the pommel. You can set up either a straight punch or a snake punch with the knucklebow (the knap will be the same as well—actually, leather gloves do wonders for unarmed knap sounds!). Just be absolutely sure the blade of the punching sword is straight up and down, point up, perpendicular to the ceiling! Watch that with the punching intention, the point does not tilt toward the victim at all.

Attack Alternatives

The ten-move drill covers most of the attacks you'll ever need for a basic rapier fight, but here are a few more to make your fight technique vocabulary complete.

Groin Strike (low 5): You can cut or thrust to the groin; just be sure (of course) to send attacking energy past your partner's body, not into it. A groin cut should lead with the knuckle edge, and a thrust can be either way. The groin or low five parry is horizontal, slightly in front of the knees; if you choose to use a reinforced low five parry, it will be identical to the staff groin parry (fig. 6.23). Watch your point when transitioning into this parry—keep the window-closing image in mind and keep your point outside your partner's body always.

Figure 6.23

Flesh Wound: Slicing your opponent is as easy as three steps: First, place the flat of the blade on the flesh in question (arm is good, or leg, never the face!); then the victim places her hand over the blade; third, draw the blade away. For a slice to the cheek, flick the sword up at the proper angle, and set up the victim far enough away that the cutting sword cuts air only. Distance and victim reaction are key to the face cut. Fake blood helps too—see the Resources section for a recipe!

Spanking: Well, it's possible, and it's safe, as long as it's with the flat of the blade, on the behind, and very, very light contact, if any. Watch your point!

Kill Shot: Somebody's got to die by the sword, right? For a rapier kill shot, softly place the flat of the blade on the victim's side (fig. 6.24). The point should not touch the victim's body, but once the

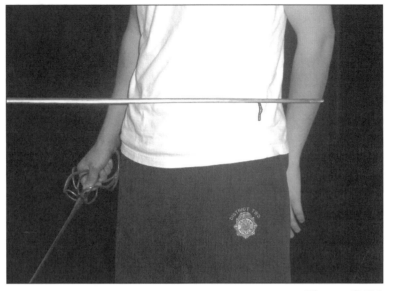

Figure 6.24

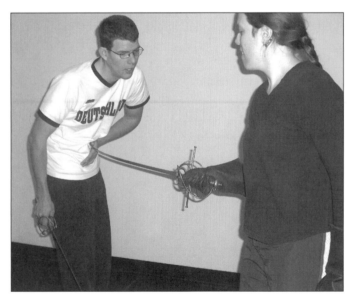

Figure 6.25

victim places his hand or elbow over the blade, the attacker should then bend the foible, with the victim's placed hand as a guide. The flexible foible will give the illusion of penetration as long as it's allowed to bend (fig. 6.25). Don't do the clichéd sword-pokes-straight-through-the-arm-at-the-side gag: It's painfully obvious, and a rapier wouldn't stab straight through a human body like that anyway.

You can use this foible-bending kill shot for any stab wound illusion as well. Do the same thing on the victim's thigh, or arm—the dramatic bending blade is a good effect to have.[10]

Disarms

Or maybe Tybalt will be a lot less threatening without his sword in hand, no? Again, there are many ways to stage a disarm; following are two of the easiest and most versatile. One thing to practice before you practice disarm techniques is how to properly drop the sword. When a weapon leaves the hand, the danger level increases quite a bit. The safest way to let your rapier go is similar in principle to the stage fall: Get it as low to the ground as possible before letting gravity take over. Hold the rapier parallel to the floor, lower it as far as possible, then drop it gently, keeping it flat as you do so. Since the rapier has a long, thin blade and substantial hilt, letting it go sloppily can result in a steel point sticking up into the air (and consequently into the actors). After the sword is on the ground, be conscious of where it is at all times—take a moment to clear it from the playing space, or move the fight elsewhere. If actors step or fall on a weapon, it's not good for the weapon or for the actors. It's also distracting to the audience.

Hilt Slam: Try this from a parry of one: Slide in close to your partner until both hilts clash together. Be sure as you slide in that your blades keep contact the whole time. Then, smack your partner's blade or hilt with your hilt. You don't have to do it very hard to make a convincing sound. Your partner should be the one in control when he lets go of the sword. Practice slowly at first, then gradually speed it up until the smack sound is in sync with the sword drop. Watch the point!

You can also use an unarmed hand for a hilt slam disarm: From a parry of one (or merely from an avoid), slap the attacker's hand or wrist. Again, don't do it too hard—you want a disarm illusion, not a real disarm! The attacker will respond to the touch by safely dropping the sword.

Figure 6.26

Figure 6.27

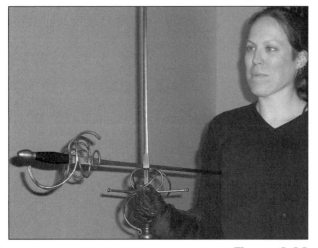

Figure 6.28

Fancy Schmancy: The attacker does a cut of three (have him help by coming in with the flat of the blade, not the edge like he's supposed to). Instead of parrying the attack, the defender catches the blade with the armpit so that it's trapped between her side and arm (fig. 6.26). Defender: Circle your blade to the right and all the way around and under the attacking blade until his middle or forte rests on your hilt (fig. 6.27). Watch your point as you circle! Then all you need to do is parry three, and the attacker's sword will leave his hand naturally (of course, he'll also let go at the right time) (fig. 6.28). You can do the Fancy Shmancy Disarm with the defender unarmed, as well.

On the Other Hand . . .

Historical rapier fencers often used either a parrying aid or another weapon in their left hand. Rapier and dagger was a common combination in the 1600s, but other objects were used as well, such as small shields, bucklers, steel gauntlets, even a weighted cloak wrapped around the hand. Using the left hand for attacks and parries is as easy as adding it to the drill you already know: Left-side attacks can be parried with the left-side object, right-side attacks with the rapier. Or just the opposite: Cross parries each time. Or parry each attack with both the rapier and the left-hand object, either a crossed rapier and dagger, or a rapier parry reinforced with a shield slam, etc. Since you've done the drill a million times by now, common sense will show how the left hand can come into play.

Other European Swords: An Overview

There are as many different styles of European sword as there are eras and cultures, from the Roman gladius to the Victorian soldier's sabre. To go into historical and technique detail with all of them would take several volumes. So here's an overview of a few different types of European sword that you are most likely to encounter in the theatre. The drills are the same (attacking and parrying the variety of body targets in order), but the size and shape of the sword will dictate how it is wielded.

Broadsword

The broadsword is an older sword than the rapier. It's large (in some cases, like the Scottish claymore, ridiculously large), two-handed, with a thick and heavy blade (see fig. 6.29). Cuts and thrusts are done the same way for stage as they are for the rapier, but with two hands. In general, a broadsword fight will be slower, given the weight of the weapons, and often the broadsword was used almost more as a bludgeoning weapon

Figure 6.29

than a bladed one, again because of its weight and size. Many instructors recommend reinforced (one hand holding hilt, one hand holding blade) parries for three, four, and five when doing the drill with broadswords.

Smallsword

The smallsword is a later sword than the rapier—in fact, the transitional-hilted rapier morphed into the smallsword by the 1700s. The smallsword is extremely light, shorter than the rapier, with a thin, needlelike blade. The smallsword was used almost exclusively for thrusting, not for cutting and pummeling. So drills and choreography for the smallsword will emphasize point play and be very fast![11]

Knives

Knives cover many different sizes depending on what time period they come from. A "main gauche" of the Renaissance is about a foot long, whereas a modern switchblade can be a couple inches. The main thing to remember about knife fights is that knives are short, so actors' safe distances will be pretty close together! Not only that, but a knife's small size means quick movement and lots of slash-and-avoid-type moves. By the time two short knives clash together, partners are very close, and basically, the fight will be over soon! An entire drill with knives is not necessarily realistic, but a circling, slash-and-avoid sequence makes a lot of knife sense. Again, use research, common sense, and the rapier drill to explore weapon differences and style differences.

1   This manual covers the fundamentals of rapier-only technique. For more history and for detailed rapier/dagger drills, see Dale Anthony Girard's book *Actors on Guard*.

2   There are several truly stage-ready blades that are épée or "musketeer" blades, but I've used both in rigorous performances and full-semester classes, and they do not hold up nearly so well as the schlager.

3   Dennis Graves and Dale Girard, respectively.

4   Thanks to Dale Girard whom as far as I know, came up with the index-card-as-sword idea first.

5   It feels similar to the staff's strike.

6   I once had a fight partner who lunged hugely! I had to literally leap and skitter away from him as he attacked. But at least I stayed in safe distance! Small folk paired against big folk: Feel free to add more footwork than your partner uses. If you're barely five feet tall and your six-foot-two-inch partner is going to lunge at you, more than just one retreat will do the trick to keep you safe!

7   This drill, and the numbers that name the moves, are from the universal rapier curriculum of the Society of American Fight Directors, who in turn adapted them from classical European fencing. Though I am not an SAFD-certified instructor, I feel that this ten-move drill is the most comprehensive rapier drill I've seen, and I use it in my own classes.

8   The overhead cut, remember, should not be an axe chop with energy down into your partner's head; it should be an illusion, flicking your energy past her head—it's actually just like a fly-fishing cast!

9   SAFD folks and fencers will know that an *envelopée* is, in fact, a giant circle as described here, and a *bind* is instead a diagonal line. For beginners, I always teach the bind as a circular motion, because it keeps the students' blades well away from faces. So in beginning classes, I always teach the term "bind" to mean any time two blades are connected and brought around actors.

10   I remember a bit of Renaissance Fest choreography that included a stab to the thigh as the victim was down on the ground. It was quite a nasty, good-looking wound illusion, and the audience in the round couldn't figure out how it was done safely!

11   I once had the honor of being allowed to hold a real live smallsword from the 1700s. It was so light, it felt like it would float out of my hand!

Chapter Seven

Asian Swords

In the European and American theatre worlds, actors will more often than not be asked to use European-style swords and techniques in stage shows. Nine combat-laden shows out of ten will use the rapier, or in some cases the older, larger European broadsword styles for sword fights.

Yet the past couple of decades (and, indeed, the past couple of years even more so) have shown a dramatic rise in Asian-style fighting in film. The *Matrix* trilogy, *Crouching Tiger, Hidden Dragon*, *Kill Bill 1 & 2*, and even such fluff action films like the *Charlie's Angels* series use more kung fu–style strikes and blocks than Western roundhouses and ring boxing. In accord with this relatively recent media obsession with Shaolin monks and ninjas, I have included this chapter as a useful overview of a generally Eastern-looking system for use in stage combat.

The Katana

Tai chi sword forms and Japanese kendo have been around as real combat arts for millennia. To truly and fully understand any

Asian-style sword system, you really should cross-train in the actual martial art itself. This chapter is a brief look at ways of wielding the *katana*, a Japanese two-handed sword popular especially in feudal-era Japan, onstage and safely. This chapter is not nor cannot be a substitute for kendo training; it is merely this author's response to a demand for a more Eastern-looking style for stage as well as an accurate inspiration for lightsaber fighting, much of which is heavily influenced by samurai lore. I am not pretending to be a kendo instructor, but I am providing safe, stage-ready drills, basic stances, etc., in case you find yourself in a production of *Hamlet* done Noh-style, or fancy yourself a Jedi.

All the techniques, stances, drills, etc. in this chapter are safe, stage-ready, made-up techniques loosely based on Japanese katana forms and the SAFD rapier drill as it pertains to targets and safety. These basics are approximations useful to convey a style onstage, and are in no way meant to be a real martial art or a cultural insult.

Weapon Requirements

Katana are usually between two and two and a half feet long, but the length (just as in rapiers of old) of the katana in real life will vary. A common and workable stage-ready length is thirty-nine inches total, and I'd recommend when using katana in shows that you have a uniform length for all katana used. The katana has a gently curved blade with a chisel-shaped tip and is sharpened on one edge (and the tip) instead of both edges, as with the rapier. This means the katana is primarily a cutting weapon.[1] The handle is topped by a *tsuba*, or guard, which is often ornate and protects the hands much like a rapier's steel hilt but in a smaller capacity. The grip is wrapped with cord and capped at the end with an ornate pommel, which fits closely to the end of the handle instead of protruding outward as with European swords. Katana are usually used two-handed, but there are some one-handed alternatives and flourishes as well.

Where to Get 'Em

Honestly, it's pretty rare to find a stage-worthy katana out there in the weaponry world. Usually those that make good katana make them for real or for wall decoration, and those who make stage swords rarely make katana. Your best bet would be to order custom katana through one of the higher-quality stage weaponry makers. It'll cost more than your standard rapier stock, but it'll be worth it. Be sure that when you're shopping for a stage katana, it's solid, with replaceable parts, and made from not-too-soft nor too-brittle steel (see chapter 6 for rapier safety standards). Those weapon emporiums which actually make or have made stage-ready katana are noted as such on the resources page in the back of this book.

For practice and beginning work, I'd highly recommend using the *bokken*, or wooden practice katana. Bokken are well balanced, made of solid wood (so are good for stage work practice), and have the same curve and movement a steel katana would, not to mention their extremely reasonable price range. Most bokken will be slightly heavier than a metal katana, but all the better for strength conditioning![2]

Conditioning

As in any sword work, using a squeeze-ball for the hands and forearms as well as the Ninja IQ Tests for wrist flexibility is always good (see chapters 4 and 2, respectively).

Another good exercise for the hands is one I learned in African-dance class: I call it the "finger doodle." Start with both palms up, then fold your fingers into a fist one finger at a time, starting with the pinky. As you fold the last fingers in, turn both hands over so your palms face down. Open the hands the exact same way, but working backward. Do this many times with different tempos in counts of five.

Figure 7.01

One Hundred Cuts

Start in the overhead stance, *daijodan no kamae*, and cut straight down until the tip of the blade is a couple inches above the ground (fig. 7.01). Practice eradicating any wobbliness as you cut, and try your best to cut to the exact same point in space every time. Plié and breathe out as the blade cuts down through the air. Do this one hundred times as a warm-up.

Another good conditioning practice with One Hundred Cuts is the horizontal cut: Start with your hands at the center of your belly, and cut straight horizontally, leading with the sharp edge and keeping the sword straight and close to your body throughout. Breathe out as the blade slices through the air, and again practice straight, swift cuts with no wobbles.

Wielding

Once you learn and are fully comfortable with the rapier drill and dynamics of keeping that variety of sword safe for stage, to do the same with other varieties of sword, even such different styles as the katana, need only adjustment, not relearning from scratch. The main difference you'll find when wielding the katana after having used European swords is the curve of the blade. This curve will influence the way you move with this sword (it should feel quite a bit more swift and controllable than a bulky European broadsword), so notice the curve and work with it as you learn.

Etiquette

Reread the Etiquette section in chapter 5 to remind yourself of the basics of general weapon etiquette. As far as Japanese sword etiquette goes, there are varied lists a mile long that are not appropriate for this manual. The following are a generic style useful for a stage look. As mentioned earlier, for true immersion in a martial art's custom and culture, study kendo or another martial art sword form.

There is a Japanese martial art called *iaido*, which is concerned solely with the unsheathing and resheathing of the katana. Imagine two Japanese samurai adversaries, sitting down to tea. One draws his katana, swipes, and resheaths fast as a wink. The other falls down dead, slashed through the heart. That's often as fast and complex as sword fights were in real life (often in European rapier fights as well), so keep that in mind when setting up katana choreography: Not much is needed! Also, there is an elaborate ritual surrounding resheathing the katana after it has been used, which also does not belong here in the fundamentals. If the show being produced is set in feudal-era Japan, in-depth research on all aspects of the setting must be studied for authenticity, far beyond what this chapter lays out.

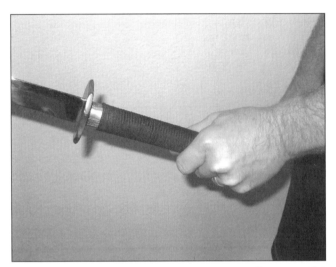

Figure **7.02**

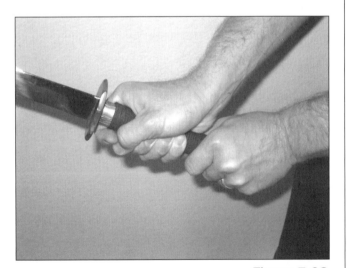

Figure **7.03**

The Bow: Not only should you bow to your weapon before the first time and after the last time you wield it, but also bow to your partner, for the same purpose as in previous chapters. If you bow to your partner with your sword in its sheath, just place your hands on your thighs and bow straight from the waist. When kneeling, place your hands in front of you on the ground and bow over them. If you bow with your sword drawn, be sure the point and "sharp" edge are directed away from your partner.

When you are ready to learn how to cut, hold the katana with both hands, the right hand under the guard, the left hand behind as added support and control. Always cut with the "sharp" edge leading. (see figs. 7.02 and 7.03).

Stances

The Japanese word for "stance" is *kamae*. So you'll notice the Japanese name for each stance ends in the phrase *no kamae*, signifying it's a stance. Again, just as in European sword work, there are as many formal stances as there are ways to hold the thing. The three stances that follow are basic, versatile, and indicative of a vaguely Asian style. Feel free, when learning these stances, to use either the Japanese or English terms as references.

Hasso No Kamae (*The Jedi*): You'll recognize this stance if you are a *Star Wars* fan: Hold the katana perpendicular to the ceiling, close to your right shoulder,[3] top elbow parallel to the floor, sharp edge facing forward. Your left foot should be slightly forward (fig. 7.04).

Figure 7.04

Seigan No Kamae (*En Garde*): Standing with the right foot slightly forward, hold the katana relaxed at the waist, pointing the tip outside where a partner's shoulder would be. Just like in the European stance of the same name, en garde can be either low or high as well (fig. 7.05).

Daijodan No Kamae (*Crazy Samurai*): Again, the right foot is slightly forward. Raise the katana above your head so that the blade is pointed 45 degrees behind. With the feet parallel, this is the stance you use in your One Hundred Cuts conditioning exercise (fig. 7.01).

Figure 7.05

Footwork

The advance, retreat, and passes forward and back are the same when wielding the katana as with wielding the rapier. Review the footwork covered in chapter 6, and practice both linear footwork and the tire pattern while holding this curved, two-handed weapon.

Cut and Thrust

Since a real katana is sharpened only on one edge, emphasis in katana swordplay is almost exclusively on cuts. The curved blade and chisel shape of the tip make even a thrust flow into an almost cut-like motion; even if you're trying to poke someone with a katana, you'll end up slicing him anyway.

The cut motion for safety onstage is very similar to the motion used with European swords (the two-handed broadsword, especially) in that all cuts are telegraphed; that is, they are extended before any leaning or footwork occurs, and the energy of the cut is sent past the partner, never into her body. Targets are still about four inches outside the body part indicated, and you should still always make sure you watch your targets. The difference in movement will be felt in the blade's curve, so feel this dynamic and work with it, making sure that your cutting movements don't curve too much with the blade's curve and end up closer than safe distance.

Try substituting your One Hundred Cuts exercise with stage-safe cuts, aimed past an imaginary partner. Feel how the katana cuts through space, and control any wobbliness you may have before putting a partnered drill together.

The Drills

I have provided three different drills to give not only good practice, but a versatile vocabulary of movements for the katana. Unlike in previous weapons-related chapters, each drill is different from the others, thereby giving both solo and partner practice opportunity, and a wide variety of moves.

Nine Cuts

This is a drill to practice alone, to get the feel for the dynamic of the katana's curved blade and the feel of the katana cut (and one thrust!) through space.

1. Cut straight down, overhead to floor (fig. 7.06)

2. Cut straight up, floor to head level (fig. 7.07)

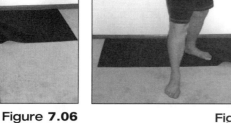

Figure **7.06**   Figure **7.07**

3.   Diagonal cut down, high L to low R (fig. 7.08)

4.   Diagonal cut up, low R to high L (fig. 7.09)

5.   Horizontal cut at waist level, L to R (fig. 7.10)

6.   Horizontal cut at waist level, R to L (fig. 7.11)

Figure **7.08**   Figure **7.09**

Figure **7.10**   Figure **7.11**

7. Diagonal cut up, low L to high R (fig. 7.12)

8. Diagonal cut down, high R to low L (fig. 7.13)

9. Thrust center (fig. 7.14)

Figure 7.12

Figure 7.13

Figure 7.14

Practice this cut series over and over until it looks like a smooth, precise sword dance. Here is a chart to help remind you as you learn and repeat.

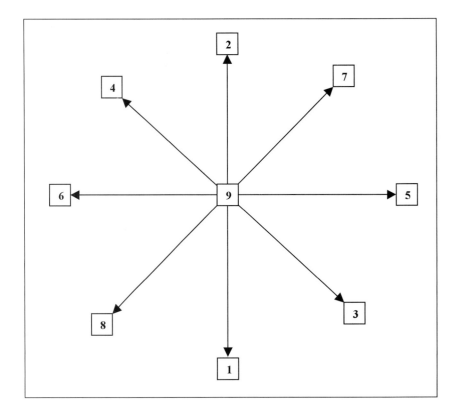

Partnered Drill

Here's a simple drill to practice with a partner: Remember, as in all safe stage swordplay, blades must always meet edge to edge and at 90-degree angles. Be sure you check safe distance first, and be sure you are merely "kissing steel"[4] and not meeting with hard impact. It is especially important to remember this rule with the katana, as the curved blade can slide dangerously if two people put too much pressure on parries and attacks together. Remember, the object is to place a parry and meet the parry lightly, energy being sent past your partner. Also as always, especially when transitioning between parries and cuts, be hyperaware of where the point of your sword is, and don't cross the plane of your partner's face (or body, except in a swipe-avoid). The partnered drill is as simple as it gets:

Attacker:

1. Cut L hip

2. Cut L shoulder

3. Cut R hip

4. Cut R shoulder

5. Overhead cut

6. Underhand (groin) cut

7. Add sword evasion attack from next section

Defender:

1. Point down, parry L hip

2. Circle point R, parry L shoulder with point up

3. Drop point down L, parry R hip

4. Circle point up L, parry R shoulder

5. Bring hilt up for horizontal overhead parry (see rapier parry 5)

6. Circle point down L, parry horizontal forward from groin (see rapier alternative: parry low 5)

7. Add sword evasion from next section

When this drill gets going fast, it's exhilarating, what with the circling blades. Be extra-careful, especially when parrying quickly, that you take the time to make those big exaggerated circles with the point each time—imagine drawing a large circle around your partner's body or in a flat plane in front of your own body. If you get too fast and too careless, it's easy to abbreviate the circular transitions and cross the attacking partner's face. Go slowly as you practice, and bring it up to speed very gradually.

Sword Evasions

Learn this cut/evasion sequence with one person wielding, the rest running through the various evasions. In a class or cast setting, make sure all actors get to do all the cuts and all the evasions. In a class setting, you may choose to have the instructor do all the cuts, and have the class practice the evasions only. After you learn and become accustomed to this series, begin to add at least one cut-and-evade at the end of each partnered drill sequence, much like we did for the staff and rapier before.

The cuts-and-evades are herein described as happening simultaneously: If you use a padded practice katana or bamboo *shinai*,[5] doing the evasions in real time is great practice for timing and actor connection, as well as spatial awareness bumped up to speed. If you are using a wooden bokken or a stage-safe steel blade, however, *always* do the cut just after the evasion begins, and check your safe distance!

The sword evasion series below describes both the attack and the evasion, separated by a forward slash (/).

Attack/Evasion Sequence[6]

1. Overhead cut/pivot body, step forward on a 45-degree angle, ending up outside attacker's sword

2. Diagonal overhead cut / Collapse to one knee (opposite knee down on ground to direction of high end of cut—e.g., attacker cuts down high R to low L; collapse and place your L knee to kneel)

3. Diagonal upward cut / deep lunge on 45-degree angle,[7] one arm above head

4. Horizontal cut to stomach / Collapse straight down à la dying Obi-Wan Kenobi

5. Horizontal cut to knees / Rapid three-step knee removal: take three steps backward, leading with the knee closest to the incoming cut[8]

6. Horizontal cut to ankles / Tuck jump, or jump and tuck legs underneath as though sitting cross-legged in the air (fig. 7.15)

7. Thrust to midsection / pivot forward just like in number one[9]

Add backward rolls away, forward rolls to attack, or (with number three) a cartwheel away to give more distance in the evasion and to add application and speed to tumbling skill practice. These can also be done with the evader's back to the attacker, or either way with the evader on her knees instead of standing. Any of these sword evasions, along with the drill, make for effective fundamental building blocks for fight choreography.

Figure 7.15

Other Techniques

The drills should cover most of what you need for an Asian-feeling fight. Keep in mind again that, unlike the rapier, katana are built for slicing and dicing, and in real life were extraordinarily sharp. This means that you won't want a lot of blade contact when putting a katana fight together—the emphasis here should be on rapid cuts and avoids, mainly. Here are a couple of useful alternatives that aren't covered by the various drills:

Disarm: The best way to clearly show a katana disarm onstage so the audience can follow the action is to start with either evasion number one or seven. From this position, the evader can smack the attacker's forearms or wrists and, the victim being in control, let the attacker react by safely dropping the sword (see chapter 6 for a safe sword-drop description). When the timing is set right, this looks effective and dynamic onstage.

Another disarm is to slide in from a low attack-and-parry (either one or two from the drill), and clash the two sword-guards together. This can look realistic; however, great care must be taken to watch both blades vigilantly as they slide in to avoid getting them caught in the costume or the hip. Be gentle with this one—too hard an impact makes for a real disarm, not a controlled one as it should be.

Killshot: The most effective killshot for the katana is not a stab but a slash to a vital area. For mid-distance kills, just have partners placed farther away from each other than standard safe distance for the drill—partners will be a bit farther apart than they are in the swipe-avoid combinations from chapter 5 or 6. The attacker should slash through the air directed at a body target (midsection level is most realistic), and the victim reacts accordingly. When done at full stage speed, the extra distance is not noticeable by an audience.[10]

A closer-range killshot works much the same way as the rapier "flesh wound": Place the flat of the blade across the victim's midsection. Since the katana will not bend like a rapier and is a slashing weapon, all an attacker need do is safely act a stage push away, slashing the air as you leave the victim's body. This can be done at arm's length or as close as a corps-a-corps. The thing to remember is: Place, then draw back. This gives the audience plenty of time to register that blade-to-flesh contact has been made, and also gives actors the safety of pulling away without anything actually getting cut.

Corps-a-Corps: As with the rapier, there are many effective and safe ways to get into a corps-a-corps with the katana: In fact, both the bind around to shoulder meeting (see fig. 6.22), and also the pommel strike-and-catch corps-a-corps we learned in chapter 6, actually can work as well with the katana. As long as you are steady and the blades themselves stay safely away from partners' faces, any crossed-sword pose can work as a corps-a-corps with this two-handed weapon (fig. 7.16).

Figure **7.16**

Especially effective and for added safety, slide in hilt to hilt for each corps-a-corps. It gets partners closer together and steadies the swords so they won't slide around inordinately.

Other Asian Styles

As mentioned before, actors in America or Europe are most likely not going to run into varied Asian-style swordplay in stage work. If you are cast in a kung fu film, the director will have more in-depth and culturally specific choreography for you. As taught above, the basic katana, in length and style, is useful for a general knowledge of the look and feel of Asian weaponry, and also for lightsabers.

Other Japanese swords differ from the katana mainly by length (the long *daito* and short *wakizashi* or dagger-length *tanto* are three size variations), and the wielding of these other swords will not be any different from what is laid out here other than distance from partner and swiftness. The *ninjato* is a sword style popular from films: It is shorter than a katana and is straight, not curved. The hilt of the ninjato is larger than a katana's and square in shape. But its use for stage combat is also nearly identical to that of the katana.

There are countless Chinese sword styles as well as other weapons both from China and Japan that have found their way into films, especially through various martial arts trends, from ninjas of the 1980s to Bruce Lee: the *sai*, *nunchaku*, chain, butterfly swords, Chuck Norris's cowboy boots, etc., all have their own complete schools and forms. For the fundamentals of stage combat, this overview will give you a solid beginning, grass-hopper. Now paint the fence . . .[11]

Closing Note: The Double Figure Eight: No overview of Asian-style weaponry could be complete without learning the classic double figure eight pattern of sword-swishing. It's not nec-essarily practical for realistic fight needs, but it does look quite exciting to an audience, and many physical jokes are possible when someone is in its throes.[12] Here's how it goes:

1. R hand: L to R figure eight

2. L hand, R to L figure eight

3. R hand, start figure eight L over L hand

4. Continue: the two figure eights should interlock smoothly

A choreographer I worked with used to like ending this flowing pattern with a physical joke: As one character would be doing this double figure eight in a flashy, quick way (often with high Bruce Lee–esque wails), the other character moves up swiftly and place one strong gloved hand at arms' length, right in the middle of the pattern, on top of his partner's crossed elbows. Try it—it's pretty hilarious, especially if the caught partner tries to feebly reach forward with his weapons.

---

[1] It is said that a well-kept katana of old could cut a man cleanly in half from crown to tail.

[2] As long as your bokken is appropriately curved and well balanced, that is.

3   All katana forms are taught only right-handed, as left-handedness was not considered in the real arts on which these forms are based. Since the katana is a (mostly) two-handed weapon, it shouldn't make too big a difference to left-handed folks to follow right-hand-dominant instructions, as you'll be holding the sword with both hands anyway.

4   Girard, *Actors on Guard*, 493.

5   See Resources section for suppliers.

6   Tanemura, *Genbukan Ninpo Bugei Fundamental Taijutsu, Vol. 1*, 39–44.

7   After lunging, use your overhead hand to begin a cartwheel to evade even farther.

8   On the second of the three steps, clap the hands into the attacker's face and hold. The intention is a scattering of blinding powder as a distraction.

9   My current instructor teaches the number seven evasion with no step forward, just a torso pivot. Try it both ways.

10   Especially if you've got a little blood pack handy!

11   *Karate Kid* reference. But you knew that.

12   Remember the knife-twirling guy Indiana Jones shot in *Raiders*? That's what I'm talking about.

Chapter Eight

Other Weapons

Especially in contemporary plays, actors may be called upon to use weapons that are not in the classical vein, either small and modern or even "improvised" (everyday objects used as weapons). There are as many alternative weapons possible for stage combat as there are human ideas for how to hurt one another.

For many unusual weapons, there are limited or no standards for choreography and skill-building,[1] so it's very important to be hyper-aware, nay, paranoid, when using any found-object weapon choices. Also, having an experienced professional help with choreography is highly recommended (and in the case of firearms, required). In other words, there aren't really any found-weapon drills in existence; it takes experience with the preceding classical weapons skills as well as creativity and dramatic know-how to use the odd weapon forms described here. Some basics, anecdotes, and guidelines will help you to begin, but definitely recruit the help of a professional as well.

Found Weapons

Two office workers are laboring side by side in a shared cubicle. It's almost five o'clock. Employee A has had too much burnt office coffee, and suddenly has a bone to pick with Employee B, who has won Employee of the Month awards for the last three months running. An argument ensues, then escalates to insults, until A slams B's hand into the desk with a tape dispenser.[2] To retaliate, B hair-pulls A over to the paper-shredder, where dramatic grappling then explodes into A smacking B across the face with a phone book.[3]

How would this scene work logistically as far as staying safe to actors and seeming plausible to the audience? The hair pull and grappling we already know from chapter 3, so there are safe techniques already set for that phrase of the fight. A tape-dispenser slam would work well if Employee A held the dispenser at a severe angle, slamming the edge onto the desk while masking B's hand underneath. A thick phone book would make a great sound if used in a shared knap with a diagonal slap technique.

The main thing to keep in mind when using normal objects as weapons is to inspect each object used to ensure that there are no loose or sharp parts, that the object is solid and sturdy enough to withstand rehearsal abuse, that the actual prop is available for as many rehearsals as possible . . . in other words, assess the object's safety just as you would an "actual" weapon. More so, actually, as most everyday objects aren't constructed to the safety specs of stage-safe swords or martial arts supply staffs. Figure 8.01 shows two students in a corps-a-corps using twigs as prop wands for a Harry Potter scene, an instance of found weapons standing up well to vigorous treatment.

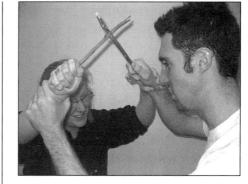

Figure **8.01**

Techniques used for a staged fight with found weapons will vary depending on the size and shape of the object used, and how big or small a moment the fight needs to be within the construct of the play. Othello's smothering of Desdemona with a pillow (found object) is the climax of the character's and the play's journey, and so should be a visible, realistic, and poignant bit of violence.

A good way to discern what technique is appropriate for found weapons is to match the object as closely as possible to a set classical weapons system you're already familiar with. The office products mentioned at the beginning of this section were matched up with the unarmed techniques that made the most sense for the size and shape of each object chosen. Two students at Metro State College of Denver, having learned unarmed, quarterstaff, and rapier techniques, composed a fight scene between two janitors, substituting long push brooms for staffs, while toilet plungers turned backward became cup-hilt rapiers. Their scene included many objects one would commonly find in a janitor's arsenal, and included even such unarmed adaptations as spraying bleach (really water) into the eyes with a spray bottle, a choke bit with a length of toilet paper, and the head-slam technique ameliorated by the use of a plunger. Another example of creative use of found weapons is a fight scene from the film *Romeo Must Die*, in which Jet Li's character defeats a group of thugs with nothing but a handful of plastic zip ties.[4] The sky's the limit, as long as safety is kept in mind always. It should be anyway!

A note regarding breakaways: Breakaway chairs and bottles are fun, but in case of the former, be sure the actor using it knows how to do safe stage falls very well, and has the opportunity to rehearse with the actual chair over and over again. Special care should be taken in the latter case: The classic hit-on-the-head-with-a-bottle-that-shatters is exciting visually, but even though breakaway bottles are made to be safe, shards can still get in the eyes or cause slip hazards if not cleaned up properly. Under no circumstances should anything other than professionally made breakaways be used at any time. Do not construct homemade breakaways for budgetary reasons—much better to go without, or go with an alternative technique.

Throwing Weapons

Since stage combat is the illusion of violence, obviously the dagger-throw technique described below is the illusion of throwing. The audience thinks it's seeing what isn't actually happening through the actors' misdirection, much like the focus-directing tricks a stage magician might use to mask an illusion.

Thrower: Hold the dagger by the blade, hilt turned toward your own body, pointing at the "target" on your partner with the weapon windup and also your unarmed hand. This will ready the audience's focus. Whip the dagger as though you have thrown it at the target—in reality, keep the arc of the movement going until you have brought your arm down to your side and have flipped the weapon round in your hand so that the hilt lies discreetly along the inside of your forearm. If the dagger isn't completely invisible, don't worry—the audience isn't looking at you anymore.

Throwee: Begin by holding a matching weapon discreetly along your forearm, hidden by your side, the blade clutched in your fist and the hilt pointed up toward your elbow. In sync with the "throw" of your partner, flip the weapon up in your hand so that you have placed your fist (not the point of the dagger, please) on the "target" body part: Your fist will cushion the point, and the weapon will protrude disturbingly straight out. This is an especially effective trick with a little fake blood in the fist. When timed correctly, the audience follows the pointed action, never noticing that nothing is traveling through the air at all.

Variation: The throwee does exactly the same reaction, only instead of placing the dagger on the body, place it in the air (just outside the face is good)—it will look like you've caught it midair, like a ninja!

A brief rant: Don't do this throwing illusion with a sword! The ridiculous spear-thrown rapier move has been done in too many films—rapiers don't move through the air like spears, and certainly don't land point first in a victim's body![5]

Swords can be thrown and caught, however, under tightly controlled circumstances. Say one character gets disarmed in a fight, and her friend/bystander tosses her a sword to help her out. This is difficult to do with most types of sword: A katana's curved blade interferes with its controlled trajectory, and a rapier hilt is small and very difficult to catch safely, especially one with a knucklebow. The European broadsword with a simple cross-hilt[6] is the type of sword most conducive for the following sword-toss trick.

Thrower: Wait until the last possible second to gently toss the sword's hilt first to a low safe target just outside the catcher's body. Your throw should keep the sword as horizontal to the ground as possible. **Catcher:** Slap-catch the sword by the grip, palm down. This way, when you miss, the weapon will fall flat to the ground. Watch carefully and don't follow the sword to try to catch it again if you miss once—let it fall. Make sure you have your leather sword gloves on, and it's a good idea to set a vocal cue between you and the thrower, so it's not left to visual timing alone.[7]

Mismatched Weapons

A rapier doesn't always have to fight against a rapier, or a staff against a staff. The techniques and drills already learned can mix and match when pitting different types of weapons against each other. The biggest safety caution is to check safe distance dili-gently—a quarterstaff has a much longer reach than a switch-blade. Be sure, when pairing different-sized weapons, that actors don't get too close for safety or too far apart for realism. Always measure safe distance by the longer weapon. Some ideas for mis-matched weapons include:

Rapier versus Staff: Use oak and steel together for maximum safety—if a rattan staff is necessary, be sure all parries with the rapier are super-light contact. Do either the rapier drill or the staff drill with both.

Rapier versus Dagger or Knife: How do the longer and shorter blades move differently? Do the rapier drill with both—or try a cut-to-the-arm disarm and end up with unarmed versus rapier and dagger. How about rapier and katana—how would Zorro fare against Musashi?[8]

Katana versus Staff: Again, use an oak staff against a blade. Try the katana drill with the staff doing reinforced blocks.

Unarmed versus Anything!: All directions of evasion, as well as rolls and falls, are useful here. Disarm to change who is armed, or disarm to turn the fight into unarmed versus unarmed.

Found Weapons versus Anything: Be sure that if you do, say, tape dispenser versus rapier, the "normal" object can stand up to the stage weapon.

Other Weapons

Unlike found weapons, there are strict set standards (and even laws) regarding the use of the following three weapons, particularly the latter two. Whips, firearms, and any pyrotechnics may not be used with this manual alone. There are severe dangers, complex handling skills, and stringent laws surrounding the following forms of staged violence. By no means should anyone try these forms without the direct supervision of professionals. Don't try this at home, kids!

Whips

Distance and victim reaction are the two building blocks that make up effective whip use onstage. Oh, and knowing how to crack a whip properly.[9] For a ten-foot whip, actors must be at least thirteen feet apart for safety. This is not a circus trick of snapping cigarettes out of the mouth; lots of distance is necessary. In a lecture/demonstration, Geoff Kent stood on one end of a large stage and I stood all the way on the other end. He cracked the whip, I reacted. The huge amount of distance between us mattered not a whit, as the large movement and sound of a cracked whip is enough to bridge the gap of distance into an illusion of an actual hit. If you need to trip someone with a whip, never attempt to crack a whip around an actor's limbs.[10] Instead, use the same principle as tripping with a staff: Place the weapon on the floor, let the victim move her leg aside, bring the weapon through where the limb used to be, let the victim safely fall. When done at speed, it can look as spiffy as anything Indiana Jones ever did.

Firearms

This branch of weapons use must be done with extensive training under the supervision of at least two professionals following the rules and laws summarized below. Even if you are using a "reproduction" gun, i.e., one that doesn't function or discharge, there are still laws surrounding its use and possession. Pay attention to these rules and regulations, and don't try any of this alone:[11]

- You are required to have a fight director with experience in firearm use, a gun specialist professional, and a fire marshal present any time guns are used. Specialists can include: theatrical armorers specializing in firearms, police or military personnel, or another equally qualified professional. The fight director is there to show how to properly handle the firearms and to give safe choreography. The gun specialist is there to know how the guns work and can be present to set the firearms for use and correct any misfires or other mechanical problems. The fire marshal is there in case anything catches fire.

- A *theatrical firearm* looks like a gun and shoots like a gun, except that instead of ammunition, it shoots blanks. Theatrical firearms are not built to discharge projectiles at all; however, severe burning and even fatal injuries have resulted in blanks misfiring or actors being too close to the weapon.

- A *reproduction firearm* looks like a gun but doesn't shoot anything at all. It is not made to discharge even blanks, though it may or may not have moving parts. Even toys are considered reproduction firearms.

- All weapons used in class or production, whether they can shoot or not, must be registered through local police. You may not even show a firearm (reproduction or no) in a public place without first contacting the police.

- Before deciding to use a firearm, the professionals you hire must do a thorough safety assessment, covering the possible hazards below and contacting the police. Warnings must appear in programs for any shots fired in a theatre to keep heart-delicate or otherwise easily startled audience members safe. Hearing protection may be necessary for actors near the discharged firearm.

- Possible hazards when using theatrical firearms include: dangerous bits and/or loud noises emanating from the gun, late or off firing, actors getting burned, deafened, or inhaling smoke, scared or startled audience members (this can cause heart attacks and/or lawsuits), and fire hazards to costumes or sets.

- People must be kept out of the firearms' range of damage. This doesn't mean only in front of the barrel, but also to the sides and underneath the weapon, as misfires and burns are possible.

- Blanks are "dangerous in the extreme"[12] and should not be used unless by highly qualified professionals. Severe burns, bits of wadding shooting out as projectiles, or a delayed misfiring can all be very hazardous. Fatal accidents can and have occurred when using blanks.[13] Theatrical firearms should be treated as though they were as dangerous as real guns. It's the same premise as using a steel stage sword—though meant for safe stage use, these are weapons, not toys.

- Squibs are even more seriously dangerous. A squib is a tiny explosive set into a special vest that can be set off by the actor wearing the vest, looking for all the world as though she has been shot through.

Look at the Resources section for the professionals to book or instruct. As far as firearms go, think twice and three times before deciding you need a theatrical firearm in your show. It's sticky, dangerous business.

I'm Burning!

No, you're not—not without a licensed professional in pyrotechnics. That's all. Nope, I'm not even going to describe how any of the partial or full burns work. Not only am I not a licensed professional in pyrotechnics, but this type of stunt—it is more than mere stage combat—is not something just anyone can or should do. The quality organizations listed in the Resources section will no doubt have a handful of pros who know lots about burns and other fire effects for stage. But the stunt performers at the Ring of Steel[14] won't even rent this equipment out to anyone without one of their professionals to perform the stunt as well. So, as has been reiterated many times before, this is advanced, elaborate stuff that ninety-nine out of a hundred staged fights will not need.

Conclusion: Stunts or Stage Combat?

Most of the stunt work seen in the movies is between difficult and impossible to produce onstage. In film, fights are spliced, edited, and (usually) set up in small chunks instead of a full fight performed all at once. Camera angles mask the safety setups, and often extra safety measures (such as crash pads) can be there just offscreen. Sounds are added in postproduction. Often actors are on wires for added effect. In the theatre, fights happen in real time; they must be positioned correctly to mask any safety measures; sounds must be realistic both in quality and in timing; and all fights must look real to a live audience, without excess padding, elaborate setups, or possibility for do-overs if something goes wrong. While stunt performers must know the preceding fundamentals of stage combat—the standards for safety and verisimilitude are universal—just know that stage fighting and fights onscreen are different monsters.

A final note regarding improvisation: As you work through piecing together various learned techniques to make fights come alive onstage, as well as creating ways to use perhaps unusual weapons or nonweapons in fights, you'll no doubt have noticed the call-and-response dynamic of stage combat scenes. Fights are merely physical conversations that happen after all words have been used up, and characters have no choice (or so they feel) but to resort to physical violence. Creativity as well as dramatic logic work together when creating illusions of violence for the stage,[15] but at no time should actors be allowed to make fights up as they go along, or "just spar" in place of choreography. Of course, partners may slowly piece together and invent scenes of their own, and obviously all realistic staged fights must look extempore to an audience, but remember: It's the characters that are improvising what happens next, never the actors.

---

[1]   Firearms are not considered found weapons, but are in a category all their own, and do have many rules for use.

[2]   One of those heavy office ones filled with sand.

[3]   This was a real fight made as part of an SAFD class—an actor named Charlie and I choreographed this (largely autobiographical) scene together and performed it for the class back in 1996. Instructor: Timothy Tait.

[4]   Bartkowiak, dir., *Romeo Must Die*, 2000.

[5]   Or stick, quivering, into a pirate ship's mast.

[6]   One simple crossbar across the top of the grip; a large rounded pommel is also good.

[7]   When I did this at our local Renaissance festival, my partner's cue to me was, "Sword!!!" And I only caught it successfully half the time, I might add. So don't feel lame if you miss in performance—it's still a cool move, and the weapon is readily available after dropping for the next part of your scene.

[8]   Both legendary swordsmen of Mexico and Japan, respectively.

9   It's all in the wrist, and it takes practice to feel it—in a very wide-open space!

10 Some whip experts are able to do this without harm to the victim—but not in the fundamentals. It takes years of experience to be able to wield a whip like this. Whips are specialty weapons and should not be played with without direct supervision by an expert.

11 Ferguson, "Weapons in Production," *Fightdirector.com*, 2001, *www.fightdirector.com*.

12 *www.fightdirector.com*

13 A moment of silence for Brandon Lee.

14 Most stunt performers will no doubt do the same, as stunts of this type are extraordinarily dangerous. *The Ring of Steel*, 2006, *www.ringofsteel.org/overview.html#fire*.

15 See chapter 9 for more details.

Chapter Nine

Don't Try This at Home

The techniques contained in this book should give both beginners and professionals a solid background in the fundamentals of stage combat without being a substitute for having a fight director present for class or choreography needs. Hopefully by now teachers and directors can go through basic stage combat vocabulary without breaking any actors, and actors have some line of defense the next time a clueless director tells them to "just use a real slap in this scene."

Many actors will do dangerous things, putting themselves or other cast members at risk just because they don't know any better and don't want to put off anyone potentially in charge of their castability. Actors: It's okay to say no. If there's anything dangerous or uncomfortable, or even just a piece of decent choreography not given enough rehearsal time, actors have the right to refuse to do such things.[1]

It's up to the actor to make sure, whether a stage combat professional is used or not, that most if not all of the following "lucky seven" precautions are being covered when stage combat or physical comedy is needed in a show:

1. There is a legitimate, knowledgeable professional in charge of choreography and rehearsals of said choreography.

2. There is adequate rehearsal time set for all choreography—one to four hours of rehearsal for each minute of choreography is standard practice. For illusions of violence, rehearsal hours should be on the high end of this rule.

3. The choreography should be rehearsed as much as possible on the actual stage and set. All choreography must be run through on the set at least once at half-speed before every performance.

4. The choreography is within the realm of possibility for an actor to perform. Challenging is good, but all actors should know their body's limits and should inform the director of any chronic injuries or problems that could influence what she choreographs for them.

5. Maintaining an atmosphere of respect and trust is your main priority when setting and rehearsing scenes of violence.

6. Any weapons used are high quality, made for stage use, and in use for all rehearsals and performances.

7. Costume pieces and any belts or sheaths for weapons are available for rehearsals as soon as humanly possible, and should be the same ones as will be worn onstage in performance.

Choreography Tips

All the techniques shown in this book are movement vocabulary. Put a few words together and you have a sentence, right? Not really.

When creating a physical bit for stage, look at who the characters are. (Look at the actors too—physical dynamic and distance play a part, as well as character.) What is each character's objective? Why is violence necessary in this scene? At what point does communication break down between the characters, where resorting to blows is the only option? How do you want the *physical dialogue* to work to further the action?

Physical Fit: Let's say you'd like to begin a fight with a punch to the jaw. Set up the safe choreography, watch the actors do it. Now notice where the actors end up physically—what is likely to happen next from this position? The one who has been punched will no doubt be hunched over and turned away from the attacker, and the attacker might have his arms raised a bit with follow-through. Does the victim see an opening in the attacker's ribs and tackle him to the floor? Does she come back with a similar blow to the face? See where the moving puzzle takes the choreography to the next step. This can be done just by visualizing as well—instead of organically choreographing onto actors, visualize this same process: Where do actors end up with each step? Set up the steps and bring them into a rehearsal or class, changing anything that doesn't work physically as well as it did in your head.

Emotional Fit: If one character has just been punched in the jaw, the fight may be over right then. If this is a comedic or fantasy-heroic-style fight, she may not have felt a thing. It will all depend on who the characters are and what sort of play they're

Figure **9.01**

appearing in. A contemporary dramatic domestic violence scene may need just the one devastating punch to give the proper effect. A Restoration comedy master-and-servant scuffle may need many more moves. See what works for the dramatic build of the play and what makes sense for the characters' objectives. Divide the fight choreography up into *phrases* to coincide with the scene's emotional *beats*.

Structural Integration: Serious fights, depending on where they appear, may not need more than one or two actual violent moves. A comedic fight will, like a good joke, often adhere to the magic "Rule of Three" repetitions. Realistic dynamics will make a piece of violence look real to the audience; exaggerated or opposite dynamics, though plausible in setup, will cause laughter in an audience. For example: A small person throws a punch at a large person that sends the large person flying across the room. Since this is the opposite reaction to what would happen in real life, this dynamic can cause laughter. An example of the exaggerated dynamic is the scene in *The Princess Bride* where the standard-sized Westley rams his shoulder into the huge André the Giant, who doesn't react even the slightest bit. Andre's solidity is being exaggerated from a real-life reaction, so this too can cause laughter.[2]

Match the Word to the Action—The Groin Kick: Because kicking a male in the groin is such a devastating move in real life, it often causes laughter onstage whether it's meant to or not, which is why it's often used in comedic scenes. If you're choreographing a dramatic rape scene and you'd like your heroine to stop her perpetrator with a kick to the groin, care must be taken with the actor's reaction. A high-pitched voice is actually the opposite of reality: When a body is struck with force, the voice will drop to the center of pain. So a man kicked in the groin will either make no sound at all (he may have the wind knocked out of him) or emit a low grunt. Since this particular move hurts so badly in reality, often nervous laughter will out no matter what precautions you take. Just be sure, when piecing together violent moves, that you notice how serious the violence would be in reality, and let the physical dialogue carry the action of the play as much as the spoken dialogue does. Choreographers of stage combat are playwrights of movement!

Here's a funny bit for a comedic groin-kick scene: Two male characters (A and B) are fighting. Both end up simultaneously kicking each other in the groin (this can be the climax of a rule-of-three repeated groin-kick joke). Both stop short and bend over the pain, hands on knees, facing downward. One or both may call "Time out!" and pause to allow the audience to respond.

Figure **9.02**

> **A:** Are you okay?
>
> **B:** Yes . . .
>
> **A:** *(looking up)* I wasn't talking to you.
>
> *Rim shot*[3]

A Brief Tangent: "Wire Fu"

The popularity of putting actors in a harness and flying them through the air in many film fights has prompted some of my students to ask about this sort of thing as it relates to fighting onstage. Many actors are wire-happy after seeing such contemporary fight classics as *The Matrix* or *Crouching Tiger, Hidden Dragon*.

Again, it's a question of what illusions one can pull off onstage as opposed to what one can do with film. Though *Peter Pan* is a classic stage show with flight needs, usually aerial work and stage combat don't mix onstage as well as they can on film. There are three main reasons why: First, to hoist an actor into the air takes much practice, know-how, expensive equipment, and many available, qualified stage staff besides just the guy who gets to fly. Second, the danger factor goes (hopefully not literally) through the roof when an actor leaves the stage, particularly when said flight is not under his own control (as with a flight harness). Third: weapons and flying put together? Oh, the liability!

This is not to say that aerial work is impossible to pull off onstage, just that it's much easier to pull off well on film: Editing allows for short chunks to be shot at separate times, better masking of any wires or apparatus that might be visible, and even use of stunt doubles to minimize actorly liability. Onstage, it's the actor flying, not a double. The apparatus must be worn throughout or discreetly put on and off at reasonable, real-time moments. Any awkwardness or mistakes can't be done over, and any flight apparatus must either be sufficiently masked or be a vital part of the set or costumes that won't jar the audience out of suspension of disbelief.

Then there's the formidable task of getting fights in the air while still looking good. Disney's stage version of *Tarzan*, which opened on May 10, 2006, used extensive aerial work, including Jane suspended above the stage in a net, menaced by a "spider"; Tarzan himself entering swinging on a vine from a mezzanine, a "butterfly" swooping above the audience, and other flight-harness pieces. Reviewers didn't mention any aerial combat scenes, but did express chagrin, both at the clunky style of flight and the poor sightlines. Jacques LeSourd didn't think the harnesses were a good technique for the show. He said, "Oddly, this kind of flying emphasizes the power of gravity instead of making it disappear. The actors droop when they should float."[4] Not what you want to see when watching *Tarzan*.

Aerial Anecdotes

Peter Pan: In an early scene, Peter flies in to the Darling children's bedroom, then ends up flying back out the window with all of them. Do all the flying actors have to be attached to wires the entire scene? The audience would definitely end up seeing and being distracted by the wires if so. The playwright has done a brilliant thing with this wire-on, wire-off problem: All actors who fly have their harnesses on, but the wires get clipped on and off by stage hands each time the characters declare they "hear someone coming." So the actors can go hide behind curtains/in bed and secretly get wired on or off depending on what's needed.

At a production I participated in at Boulder High School in 1989, there was in fact a stage combat scene that also used flight. Peter Pan, dagger in hand, was to fly up to the topmost platform of the pirate ship to menace Captain Hook. So he was flown up, only to come up short and bash himself on a piece of pirate ship, right in the groin. This is what can happen when an actor is not in control of his own locomotion.

Figure 9.03

Flying Vampires: There was a fight scene in Frequent Flyers Productions' *Theatre of the Vampires* that included aerial aspects. Since this show was an aerial dance piece, the problem of the audience seeing the flying apparatus was unique: The low-flying trapezes were, in fact, visible constantly during the show, and the dancers' prowess in using them made the apparatus more an integral part of the set than anything that needed to be masked. By the time the fight scene came up at the end of Act One, the audience was accustomed to seeing the trapezes constantly. The fight itself was unarmed and exaggerated in slow-motion, so actors were not simultaneously swinging in the air and swinging at each other, but rather used the trapezes as escape routes after the fight was over. In another scene, a dancer hung by the hips on a trapeze while another one climbed down the ropes to vampire-bite her. They worked with shared weight (as in contact improvisation, when two dancers give each other their weight—ballet lifts and the like), in order to ensure that her skin would not be in danger as they spun together.[5]

Aerial dance using low-flying trapezes is a great cross-conditioning program, incidentally. What was once a rare and wonderful style of performance has now shown up more and more in the wake of Cirque du Soleil's popularity: There are two prominent aerial companies in my neck of the woods, besides the aerial classes required for the Denver Center Theatre Company's MFA acting program. The training creates sustained, fluid strength, releasing work for a combination of relaxed and energized movement, as well as spatial awareness big time! Also, the seamless movements from floor to moving apparatus to air and back to floor are excellent training for stage combat's falling and rolling dynamics and core strength.

Figure 9.04

In general, though, "wire fu" or stage combat with aerial components is best left to the film professionals. Aerial work can be an added benefit to a stage show, but only if done right, by qualified professionals, depending on how the flying apparatus is used and integrated throughout. Also, to be cast in a show with aerial components, extensive supplemental training is required. Extra rehearsals and training is needed even for a simple flying harness.[6]

Conclusion

Actors should never find themselves uttering the words, "It's okay, it didn't hurt that much." Directors should never utter the phrase, "Go ahead and just slap him in this scene." Stage combat is an essential skill set for all theatre practitioners, for safety's sake, if nothing else. Stage combat choreography (and it should always be choreography, never sparring or improvisation) should look realistic to an audience, feel energetically compatible with an actor's intentions, and be completely safe at all times.

Hopefully this manual has given readers insight into what goes into the physical training and dramatic contexts of learning and creating illusions of violence for the stage. For more information, research, professionals or equipment for hire, and other opportunities for continued education about the art of stage combat, check out the Resources section of this book. Have fun and stay safe!

---

[1]   For Actor's Equity rules concerning stage combat and actors' rights, contact your local AEA chapter, or refer to Girard's *Actors on Guard*.

[2]   Reiner, dir., *The Princess Bride*, 1987.

[3]   Druyor, Kent, Zukowski, and performers, *Enough Talk, We Fight!*, Colorado Renaissance Festival, 1997.

[4]   Jacques LeSourd, "*Tarzan* Swings . . . and Misses," May 11, 2006, *http://nl.newsbank.com*.

[5]   Smith, dir., *Theatre of the Vampires*, Frequent Flyers Productions, 1997–8.

[6]   I was in classes twice a week for two years before I was cast in a bit part in FFP.

Resources

The following is a collection of various resources for research, educational, and shopping needs in the field of stage combat. This list is by no means exhaustive, nor are the organizations included affiliated with me or this book. If you are purchasing weapons from any of the suppliers listed below, it is your responsibility to check and double-check to make sure all weapons are safe before using them, and to use them in a manner appropriate for their make. I have not used equipment from many of these suppliers, and cannot be held responsible for any information or equipment obtained from any of these sources.

Stage Combat

Instruction: (See also some supply sites and research sites below that offer instruction.)

The Academy of Theatrical Combat:

www.theatricalcombat.com

The Society of American Fight Directors:

www.safd.org

Andrew Villaverde:

www.fight-direction.com

Jenn Zuko Boughn:

bonzuko@hotmail.com

Supply:

Forte Stage Combat:

www.fortecombat.com

Rogue Steel:

3738 Blanchan Ave., Brookfield, IL 60513

roguesteel.com/index.html

Dennis Graves, sword cutler:

255 S. 41st Street, Boulder, CO 80303, (303) 494-4685

Preferred Arms:

www.preferredarms.com (They have katana!)

Purpleheart Armoury:

www.woodenswords.com

Research:

The Ring of Steel:

maniac.deathstar.org/groups/ros/index.html

Fightdirector.com:

www.fightdirector.com

HistoricalWeapons.com:

www.historicalweapons.com (Arms and Armor from the Past)

Stunts:

The Stuntmen's/Stuntwomen's Associations:

www.stuntmen.com, www.stuntwomen.com

Asian Martial Arts

Instruction: Finding a martial art in your area that's right for you is a personal endeavor. If you are interested in pursuing a martial art, research and studio visits come first—then it's a life-long commitment! I won't presume to list even a selection of martial arts instructors, as such a list could be endless!

Supply:

Sakura Martial Arts Online:

www.sakuramartialarts.com

Century Martial Art Supply:

www.centuryma.com

Bu Jin Design:

www.bujindesign.com

Bugei Trading Company:

www.bugei.com

Tigerstrike:

www.tigerstrike.com

Aerial Dance and Circus Arts

Airspace Acrobatic Arts:

www.airspaceacrobatics.com

Frequent Flyers Productions:

www.frequentflyers.org

Pirate's Dinner Adventure:

www.piratesdinneradventure.com
(in California and Florida)

The Pirates' Adventure:

www.piratesadventure.com (in Spain)
(Two aerial acts with pirate stage combat! Who knew?)

Boulder Circus Center:

4747 N. 26th St., Boulder, CO 80301

www.bouldercircuscenter.com

Other Stuff

The New York Pilates Studio:

www.pilates-studio.com

The Pilates Center (in Boulder):

www.thepilatescenter.com

Gaiam:

www.gaiam.com

(yoga equipment and more)

American Ballet Theatre's Online Ballet Dictionary:

www.abt.org/education/dictionary/index.html

Jason Boughn, insurance broker:

coloradolifeguard@comcast.net

(for questions about health and/or accident insurance)

Fake Blood Recipe:

So you want a little gore in your staged fight. The easiest (and cheapest) way to make stage blood packs is to use clear laundry detergent and red food coloring. If the blood pack will be inside the mouth or close to it, clear corn syrup and red food coloring does the trick just as well. To make simple, poppable blood packs, fill as much liquid as needed (more for body shots, less for mouth spitting action) into one corner of a plastic sandwich bag (*not* the kind with the zip closure). Tie off the bag very close to the liquid with a tight knot, so that the corner is tightly filled with liquid. Cut off the excess bag, and you've got yourself a blood pack, ready to burst! If you pop the pack in your mouth, be sure to spit out the deflated plastic (it can actually look pretty gross if you play it up).

Glossary

Battre main: parrying a rapier with the gloved left hand.

Beat: a division of dramatic text, usually measured by actor tactics or action-reaction combinations.

Beat parry: a sharp parry that knocks an opponent's blade away.

Bind: trapping an opponent's blade with a circular motion.

Boinking: filling in time by acting pain.

Bokken: wooden practice katana.

Broadsword: a two-handed or hand-and-a-half European battlefield sword, used mostly during the medieval era.

Corps-a-corps: "body to body"; when two actors come close together during fight choreography.

Daijodan no kamae: katana stance with sword raised above head.

Daito: Japanese long sword.

Diablo: a style of juggling using one ornate stick manipulated with two shorter sticks.

En garde: rapier stance with the sword held midlevel, pointed to the outside of a partner's shoulder. This stance is the same for the staff.

Foible: the weaker, more flexible third of a rapier blade, nearest the point.

Forte: the stronger, less flexible third of a rapier blade, nearest the hilt.

Goofinated: palm neither up nor down—a jab punch position.

Grip: the part of a sword's handle that is held, often wrapped with wire, cord, or leather.

Hanbo: "half staff"; the Japanese name for a three-foot staff, usually three-quarters of an inch to one inch in diameter.

Hasso no kamae: katana stance with sword perpendicular to floor and to the right side of the face (think Jedi in the first scene of *Star Wars: Episode One—The Phantom Menace*).

Hilt: the steel part of a sword that guards the wielding hand(s). Rapier variations: swept, cup, basket, ring, transitional.

Hira ichimonji no kamae: standing stance in which a staff is held straight and parallel to the ground in both hands, body upright and straight.

Hira no kamae: an unarmed stance with arms straight and at shoulder level.

Iaido: the Japanese art of quick-drawing the katana.

Kamae: see "stance."

Katana: a Japanese-style sword with a slightly curved blade. Usually used two-handed.

Knap: the sound made by either attacker or victim to add realism to a bit of staged violence.

Knucklebow: the part of a rapier that protects the knuckles. Usually seen in swept and transitional hilts.

Little John: staff stance named after the character from Robin Hood: staff held in the dominant hand, one end resting on the ground.

Low-flying trapeze: a wide trapeze with a hardwood bar and ropes meeting at one point. The bar is usually approximately five feet off the ground. Can be used for big swings or circling motion.

Moulinet: "windmill parry"; the circling of the rapier behind the head to switch parrying sides.

Ninjato: katanalike sword legendarily used by ninjas.

Objective: what a character wants. This drives the actor's motivation through a scene and carries a play's action.

Parry: blocking an attack.

Phrase: a way to divide stage combat choreography: usually a couple seconds to a minute of moves.

Pommel: the (often decorative) steel fixture at the butt-end of a sword.

Pronated: palm down.

Quarterstaff: a European-style staff, historically measured to the wielder's height. Stage combat quarterstaffs should be six feet long.

Rapier: a one-handed sword used by Europeans in the sixteenth and seventeenth centuries.

Reproduction firearm: gun for use onstage that does not discharge.

Rule of Three: comedic rule for repetition, either verbally (as with telling jokes) or physically.

Schlager: style of rapier blade with a lozenge or diamond shaped cross-section.

Seigan no kamae: katana stance with the sword held midlevel, pointed to the outside of a partner's shoulder.

Shinai: Japanese-style bamboo practice sword.

Spotting: can refer to either watching and helping a partner to make sure he doesn't get hurt, or the focus-point one uses to minimalize dizziness during a turn.

Squib: a small explosive rigged on an actor for the illusion of a real-time gunshot wound.

Stance: the still position taken before a move begins.

Supinated: palm up.

Suspension of disbelief: the audience's agreement to become immersed in the artificial reality of a play through the duration of a performance.

Sword: general term used to denote a long-bladed weapon.

Taihenjutsu: "body movement techniques"; Japanese term, mostly used in the martial arts to signify techniques involving falling, rolling, jumping, walking, etc.

Tanto: Japanese dagger.

Telegraphing: when one actor makes an obvious physical cue to another actor, showing what movement is coming next.

Theatrical firearm: gun for use onstage that discharges blanks.

Tsuba: katana hilt.

Wakizashi: Japanese short sword.

Wire fu: term used to describe film combat wherein an actor is on harness or other flying apparatus for added effect.

Zhuzh: (urban slang) to mess or fluff up a bit.

Bibliography

"Ballet Dictionary." *American Ballet Theatre* 2003,
   www.abt.org/education/dictionary/index.html.

Bartkowiak, Andrzej, dir. *Romeo Must Die*. Warner Bros.: 2000.

Boughn, Jason. "Cross-Sword Puzzles." Stage combat course
   lecture, University of Denver. 2001. Also personal
   communication, 1997–present.

Carr, Rachel. *Be a Frog, a Bird, or a Tree*. New York: Doubleday
   & Co., Inc., 1973.

Taylor, Ian, dir. *Chop Socky: Cinema Hong Kong*. 2004. Broadcast
   on IFC Channel, 25 Apr. 2005.

Fancy Foote Works Productions. *The Society of American Fight
   Directors* 2002, *www.safd.org*.

Ferguson, Carter. "Weapons in Production." *Fightdirector.com*
   2001, *www.fightdirector.com*.

Girard, Dale Anthony. *Actors on Guard*. New York: Routledge/Theatre Arts Books, 1997.

Harrop, John and Stephen R. Epstein. *Acting with Style, 2nd ed.* Englewood Cliffs, NJ: Prentice Hall, 1990.

Hatsumi, Masaaki and Quintin Chambers. *Stick Fighting: Techniques of Self-Defense*. New York: Kodansha America, Inc., 1971.

Hayes, Stephen K. *Ninja: Spirit of the Shadow Warrior*. Burbank, CA: Ohara Publications, Inc., 1980.

Johnstone, Keith. *Impro: Improvisation and the Theatre*. New York: Routledge/Theatre Arts Books, 1979.

Kent, Geoff. Personal communication through assisting various stage combat classes and demos. Denver: 1996–1998.

Kent, Geoff, dir., with Geoff Kent, Jennifer Zukowski, and performers. *Enough Talk, We Fight!* Colorado Renaissance Festival. Jun.–Jul. 1998.

Lee, Bruce. *Tao of Jeet Kune Do*. Santa Clarita, CA: Ohara Publications, 1975.

LeSourd, Jacques. "*Tarzan* Swings . . . and Misses," May 11, 2006, http://*nl.newsbank.com*.

Lessac, Arthur. *Body Wisdom: The Use and Training of the Human Body, 2nd ed.* San Bernardino, CA: Lessac Institute Publishing Co., 1978

Link, William and Richard Levinson. *ABC Mystery Movie: Columbo.* Series aired on NBC Primetime, 1971–77, and ABC Primetime, 1989–93.

Martinez, J.D. *Combat Mime*. Chicago: Nelson-Hall Publishers, 1982.

Morgenroth, Joyce. *Dance Improvisations*. Pittsburgh: University of Pittsburgh Press, 1987.

Tait, Timothy, dir., with Gwendolyn Druyor, Geoff Kent, Jennifer Zukowski, and performers. *More Metal. Less Art.* The Colorado Renaissance Festival. Jun.–Jul. 1997.

Nachmanovitch, Stephen. *Free Play: The Power of Improvisation in Life and the Arts*. Los Angeles: Jeremy P. Tarcher, Inc., 1990.

Polsky, Milton E. *Let's Improvise*. Englewood Cliffs, NJ: Prentice-Hall, Inc., 1980.

Reiner, Rob, dir. *The Princess Bride*. MGM: 1987.

"Stage Combat in the News." *The Ring of Steel,* 2006, *www.ringofsteel.org.*

Siler, Brooke. *The Pilates Body*. New York: Broadway Books, 2000.

"Stage Combat Worthy." *Preferred Arms,* 2003, *www.preferredarms.com/Nicked%20blades.htm.*

Tanemura, Shoto. *Genbukan Ninpo Bugei Fundamental Taijustu.Vol.1.* Tokyo, Japan: Hello Tokyo Co., Ltd., 1987.

The Thrown Gauntlet 2005, *http://thethrowngauntlet.com.*

Smith, Nancy, dir. *Theatre of the Vampires*. Frequent Flyers Productions. Halloween weekend, 1996–1998.

"Weapons Terminology Pages." *HistoricalWeapons.com,* 2003, *www.historicalweapons.com/otherweapons.html.*

Wolf, Tony. "Ne'er the Twain: Some Thoughts on the
Martial Arts/Performing Arts Dichotomy."
The Association for Renaissance Martial Arts 2001,
www.thearma.org/essays/twain.htm.

Zukowski, Ginger and Ardie Dickson. *On the Move.* Carbondale,
IL: Southern Illinois University Press, 1990.

Index